MW01620969

MY CURIOUS WORLD

First published in 2022 by Miles Kelly Publishing Ltd
Harding's Barn, Bardfield End Green, Thaxted, Essex, CM6 3PX, UK

2 4 6 8 10 9 7 5 3 1

Publishing Director Belinda Gallagher
Creative Director Jo Cowan
Editorial Director Rosie Neave
Senior Editors Fran Bromage, Amy Johnson, Becky Miles, Claire Philip
Designers Craig Eaton, Rob Hale, Joe Jones, Simon Lee, Emily Stalley
Cover Designer Simon Lee
Image Manager Liberty Newton
Production Elizabeth Collins
Reprographics Stephan Davis
Indexer Michelle Baker (MHB Indexing Services)

ISBN 978-1-960765-66-6

Printed in China

British Library Cataloguing-in-Publication Data
A catalog record for this book is available from the British Library

Made with paper from a sustainable forest.

littlehippobooks.com

My Curious World

Words by Sue Becklake, Camilla de la Bédoyère,
Ian Graham, Anne Rooney, and Philip Steele

Illustrations by Barbara Bakos, Tim Budgen, Ana Gomez, Leire Martín,
Mike Moran, Pauline Reeves, and Daniel Rieley

Little Hippo Books

CONTENTS

SOLAR SYSTEM

The Solar System is all around you. It is the Sun, eight planets, and everything else that moves through space with the Sun.

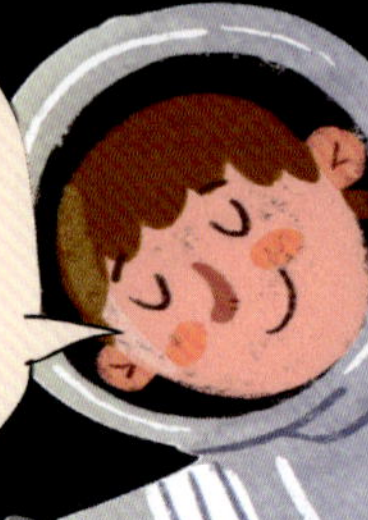

Sun

In the middle of the Solar System is a star called the Sun.

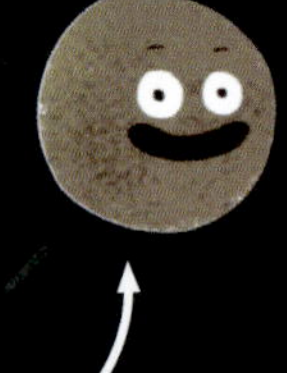

Moons

A moon is a small world that circles a bigger object—usually a planet. Earth has one, and it is made of rock.

Mercury

Planets

Planets are the giant things like the Earth that travel round the Sun. There are eight in our Solar System.

Asteroids

Asteroids are rocky worlds smaller than planets. There are millions of them.

Dwarf planets

Similar to planets in many ways, dwarf planets go around the Sun, but are not as big as planets.

Is the Sun hotter than an oven?

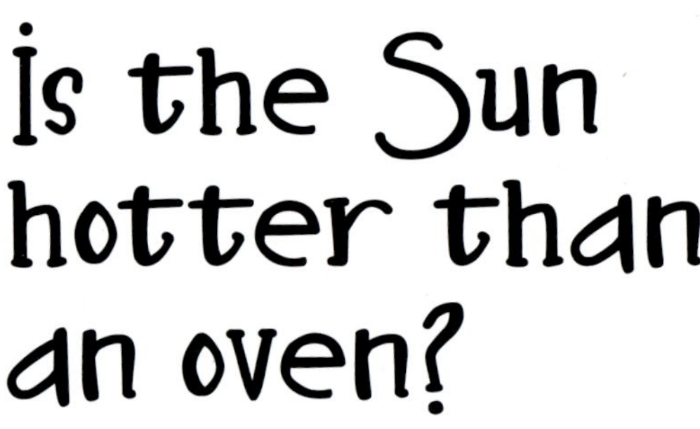

The Sun's surface is over 20 times hotter than a regular oven! The center is even hotter—thousands of times hotter than an oven. It would melt the oven!

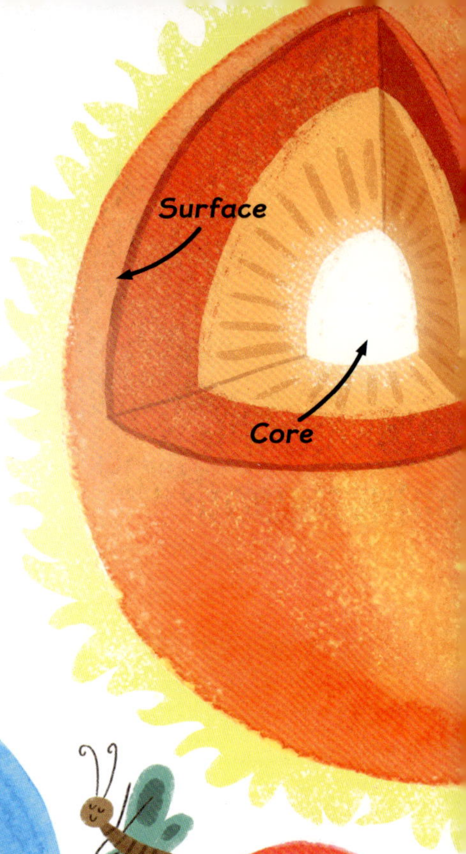

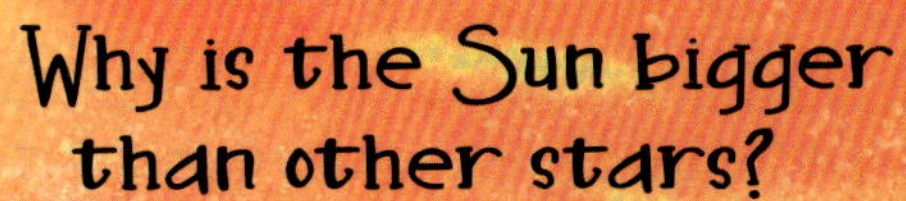

Why is the Sun bigger than other stars?

It isn't—the Sun is actually a small star. It looks much bigger than the other stars you see at night, because it is much closer to Earth than those other stars. They're all suns, but they are very far away.

Side-by-side with another star, I'm actually pretty tiny!

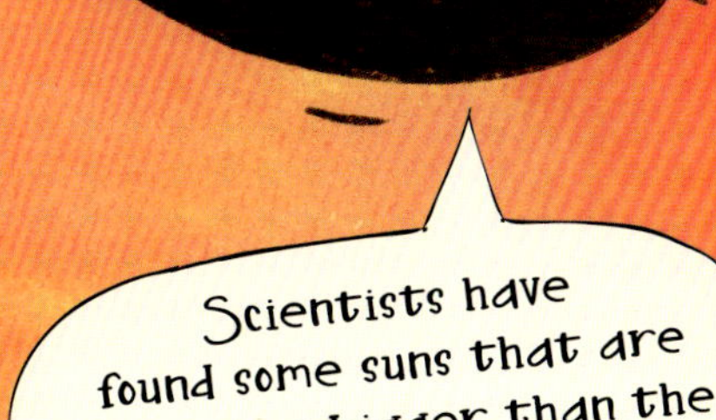

Scientists have found some suns that are 100 times bigger than the one in the Solar System!

Will the Sun be there forever?

No, but don't worry—it isn't going to disappear any time soon. The Sun should be there for another 5 billion years.

Where does the Sun go at night?

The Sun doesn't go anywhere—it's the Earth that is moving!

Our planet spins around an invisible line called the axis. It's daytime for you when the side you live on faces the Sun.

This spinning motion makes it look to us on Earth as if the Sun rises in the morning, crosses the sky, and then disappears at sunset.

Light rays

Axis

N

S

Day

Night

Sunset

ZZZ

Why is a day 24 hours long?

It takes 24 hours for Earth to spin around once, and we call this a day.

Why do we have seasons?

Because Earth's axis is tilted. This means different bits of Earth get the Sun's direct rays at different times during Earth's orbit (journey around the Sun).

What is the Equator?

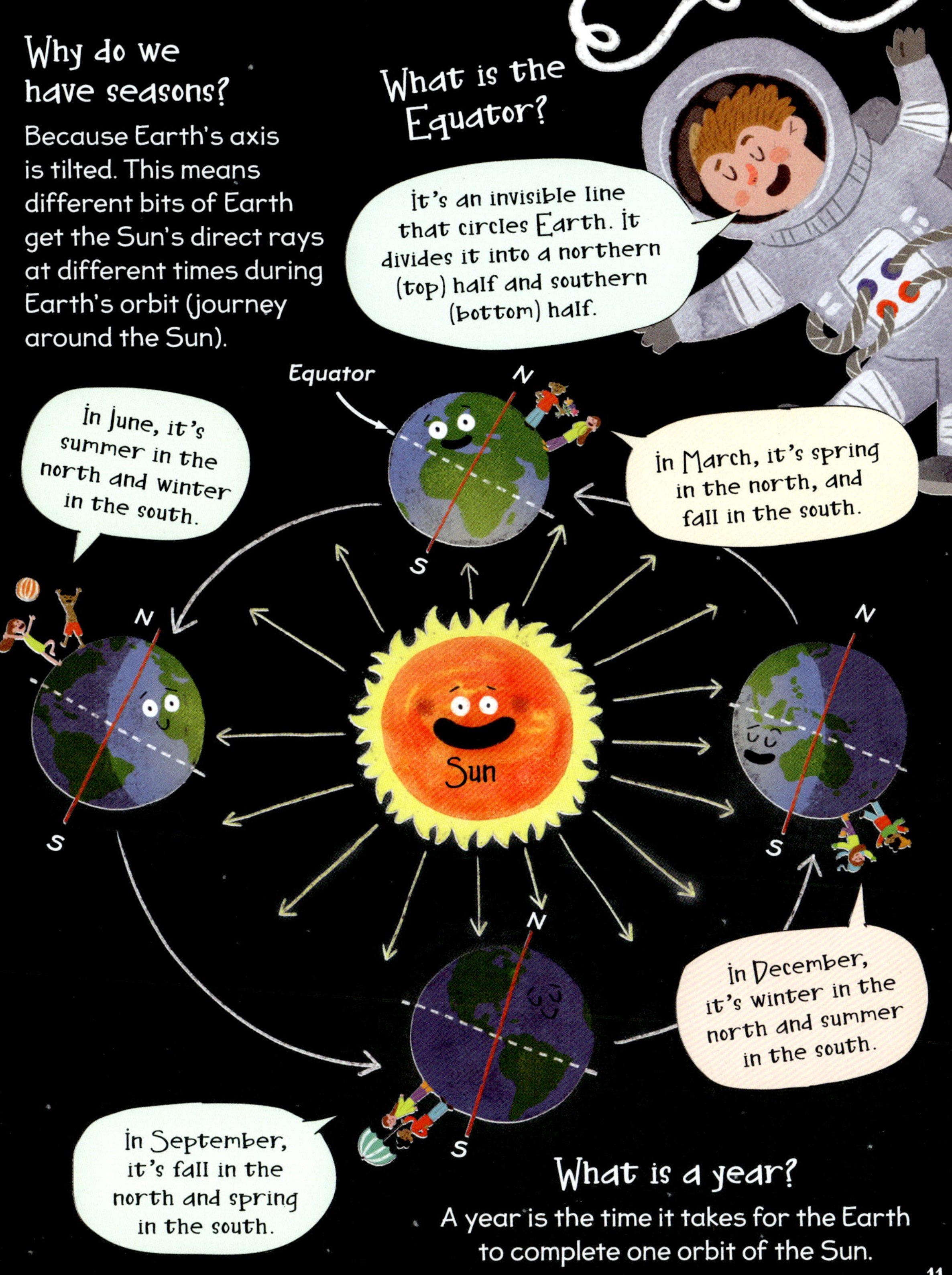

What is a year?

A year is the time it takes for the Earth to complete one orbit of the Sun.

Are other planets like Earth?

Earth and the other three planets closest to the Sun are alike in some ways, but no other planet is exactly like Earth.

Mercury is very hot because it's the closest planet to the Sun. It's smaller than Earth and it looks like the Moon.

Venus and Earth are similar in size and structure—but the two planets look very different. Venus is wrapped in thick clouds of acid. They trap heat, so Venus is even hotter than Mercury.

Water covers 70 percent of Earth's surface. Sunlight contains all the colors of the rainbow. When sunlight shines on Earth, the water reflects the blue part of the light back into space.

Mars is a small world about half the size of Earth. It looks red all over because its soil and rocks are full of rusty iron. Mars is a rusty planet.

What are the outer planets like?

The four planets farthest from the Sun—Jupiter, Saturn, Uranus, and Neptune—couldn't be more different from Earth. They are giant worlds made of gas and liquid.

Jupiter is the biggest planet in the Solar System. It's so big that more than a thousand Earths would fit inside it!

No one knows. They might have come from an icy moon that broke up...

...or they might be ice left over from making Saturn.

This blue-green gassy world was the first planet ever to be found by someone looking through a telescope. It was discovered in 1781 by a man called William Herschel (1738–1822), who became famous overnight as a result.

Both Uranus and Neptune are made mostly of water, ammonia, and methane, and it's the methane that gives them their blue color. Jupiter and Saturn are made mostly of hydrogen and helium, like the Sun.

A compendium of questions

Why aren't planets square?

Planets are round because of gravity. This special force pulls everything inward, forming a ball shape.

Why is Earth called Earth?

It comes from an ancient word meaning land. Earth is the only planet that wasn't named after an ancient Greek or Roman god.

Where is the best view of the Sun?

Standing on Mercury when it is at its closest to the Sun, the Sun would appear more than three times as large as it does from Earth.

Which moon is the weirdest?

Hmmm... maybe Saturn's moon Enceladus. It spews jets of gas and ice from its south pole!

Are there rainbows on the Moon?

Sunlight and rain are both needed for a rainbow. There is no rain on the Moon, so you will never see a rainbow there.

Why is the Earth's sky blue?

As sunlight travels through air, the blue part of the light is scattered in all directions, so the sky looks blue.

Can a spacecraft land on a gas planet?

No—and they can't fly through them either! The extreme temperature and pressure inside would crush a spacecraft.

When did the first spacecraft go to the Moon?

In 1959, Luna 2 became the first spacecraft to crash-land there—no astronauts were onboard.

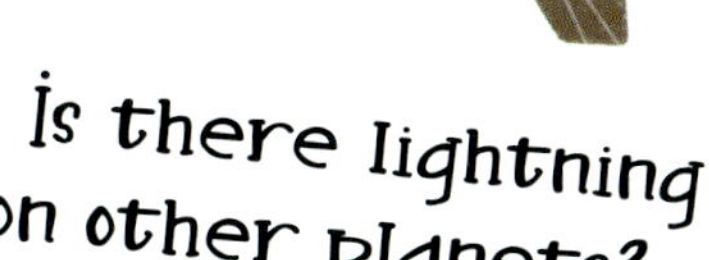

Is there lightning on other planets?

Yes. Spacecraft have seen lightning storms on Venus, Jupiter, and Saturn.

Who is the Man in the Moon?

Some people think marks on the surface look like a face. Others think they can see the shape of a rabbit.

Are all the stars part of our Solar System?

No—the Sun is our only star. All the others are outside our Solar System.

Why are the planets different colors?

Because planets are made of different mixtures of rocks and gases that reflect light in different ways.

THE MOON

A moon is a rocky body that orbits (moves around) a bigger object. Most planets in our Solar System have moons. Earth has one, which we simply call "the Moon."

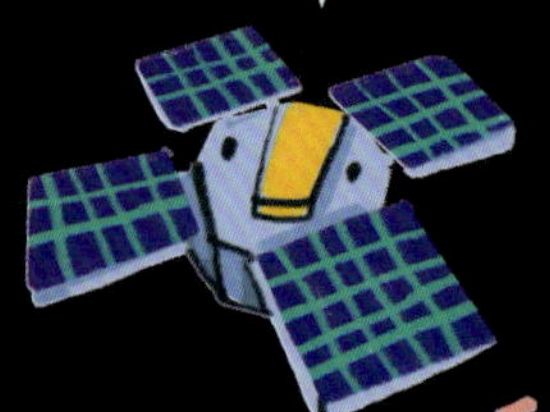

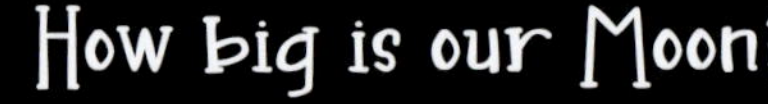

The Moon is small enough that it would fit inside Earth fifty times over. It's still the fifth biggest moon in the Solar System, though!

Does the Moon move?

It orbits Earth, and it moves with Earth around the Sun. The Moon also spins, turning on its axis (an imaginary line through the center). It takes the same amount of time to turn once on its axis as to orbit Earth once (about 28 days).

The Moon *Distance between Earth and the Moon.*

Is it far away?

Pretty far! The Moon is about 238,855 miles away from Earth. But it doesn't travel in a perfect circle, so sometimes it's a bit further away and sometimes a bit closer.

Where did the Moon come from?

It formed 4.5 billion years ago, when Earth was very new.

① A planet about the size of Mars, which has been named Theia, smashed into Earth.

② The energy of the crash melted a large amount of rocky Earth and Theia, and mixed them together.

CRASH!

4 The bits of rock whizzed around Earth, bumping into each other. Eventually, all the lumps pulled together and fused...

...making me!

What's inside the Moon?

Mostly rock. In the center, there is a small core made of metal, mostly iron. It's surrounded by a layer of hot, semi-molten metal.

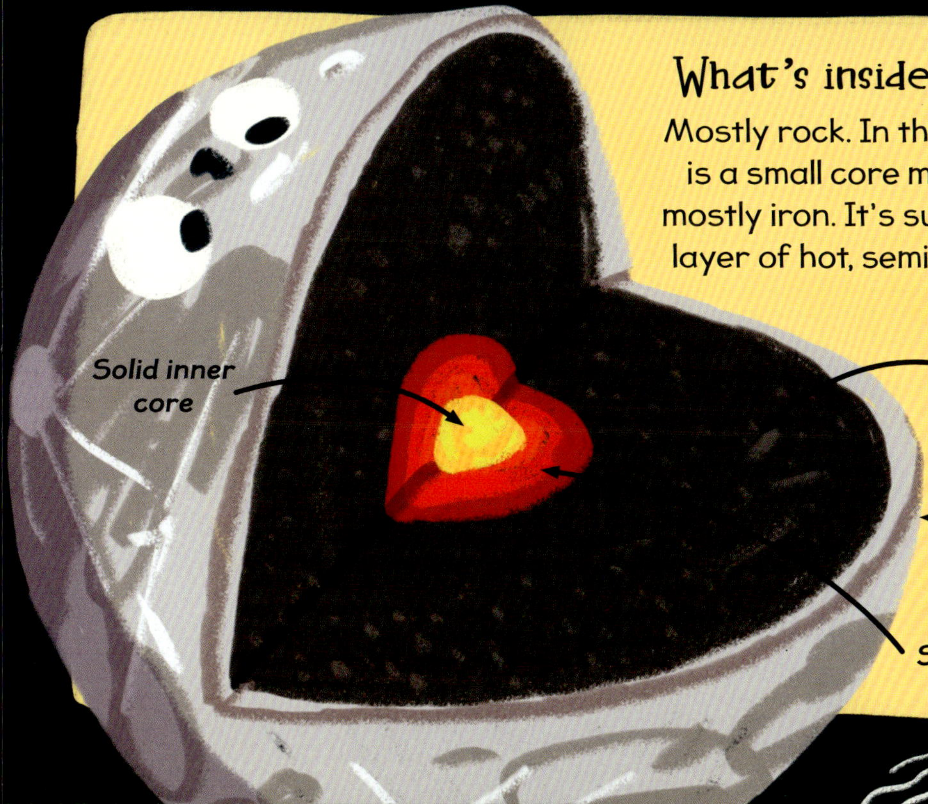

Solid inner core

Rocky mantle, semi-molten toward the core

Rocky crust

Semi-molten outer core

Why do we only see one side of the Moon?

The Moon takes as long to turn once on its axis as it takes to orbit Earth. This means the same side of the Moon is always facing us—this is called tidal locking.

What is the far side like?

It's very different from the near side. The far side has many more small craters, and even craters within the craters. It has very few flat plains, and its coloring is more irregular.

Has anyone seen the far side?

It can only be seen in photos and from space. It was first seen by humans in 1968, when the Apollo 8 spacecraft went round the Moon. A Chinese spacecraft, Chang'e 4, landed on the far side in 2019 and took the first ground-based photos.

Does the Moon change shape?

It seems to change shape, but it doesn't really. As it moves around Earth, different parts are lit by the Sun. The changes are called phases.

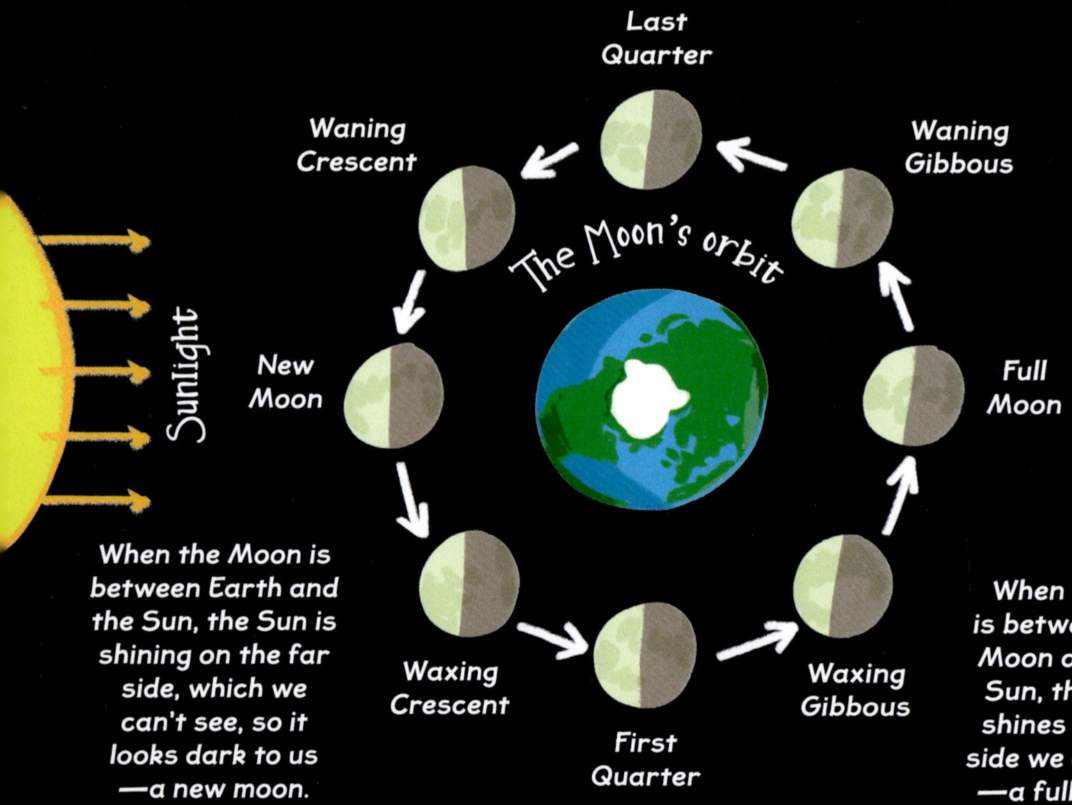

Last Quarter

Waning Crescent

Waning Gibbous

The Moon's orbit

Sunlight

New Moon

Full Moon

Waxing Crescent

First Quarter

Waxing Gibbous

When the Moon is between Earth and the Sun, the Sun is shining on the far side, which we can't see, so it looks dark to us—a new moon.

When Earth is between the Moon and the Sun, the Sun shines on the side we can see—a full moon.

Full Moon

Waning Gibbous

Last Quarter

Waning Crescent

I seem to shine because I reflect the sunlight that falls on me. I don't make my own light, like the Sun or other stars.

Why is the Moon sometimes red?

During a total lunar eclipse, the Sun is directly behind Earth and so the Moon is in Earth's shadow. Some of the sunlight passing through Earth's atmosphere is bent toward the Moon, turning it red.

Can the Moon block out the Sun?

Yes—during a solar eclipse. When the Moon moves between Earth and the Sun and they line up exactly, the Moon's shadow moves over Earth. In some places, it blocks out the Sun completely for a few minutes—a total eclipse.

Total solar eclipse

During a total solar eclipse, parts of Earth are plunged into darkness.

How does the Moon move the sea?

The Moon's gravity pulls at Earth's oceans. This makes the water pile up on the side nearest the Moon, creating a bulge. The water also piles up to make a bulge on the other side.

Most coasts have two high tides a day, one when nearest the Moon and one when furthest from it.

What causes very high and low tides?

The Sun also helps make the tides. When the Sun and Moon are lined up (at full moon and new moon), they pull in the same direction. This creates extra-high and low tides, called spring tides.

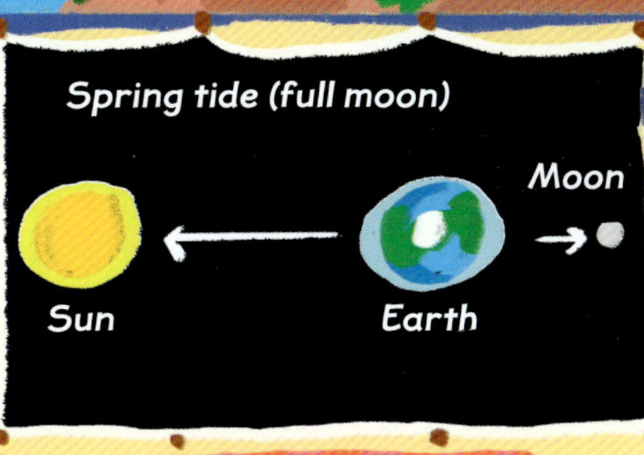

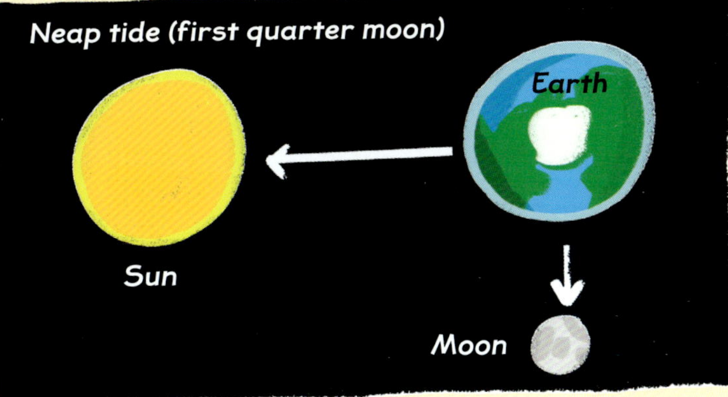

When the Sun and Moon are at right angles to each other, there are smaller tides than usual, called neap tides.

How many?

Regolith (dust) on the Moon's surface is

6.5–26

feet deep.

On the Moon, there are

500 million

craters that are more than 30 feet across.

It took Apollo 11 **51** hours **49** minutes to reach the Moon.

214

The number of known planetary moons in the Solar System.

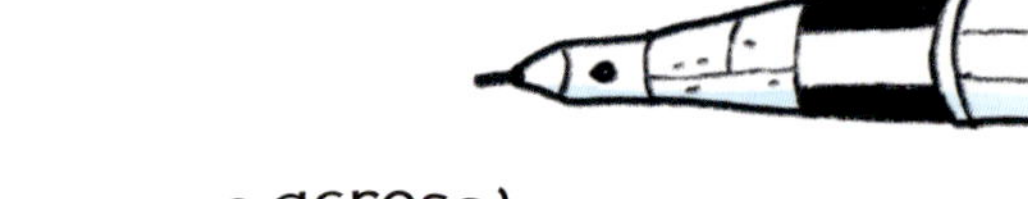

1,079 The diameter (distance across) of the Moon in miles.

12

The number of astronauts who have stood on the Moon.

Neil Armstrong spent a total of **2** hours **12** minutes on the Moon's surface (outside the lander).

Eugene Cernan of Apollo 17 spent the longest time outside the lander, a total of **22** hours **5** minutes.

The Apollo 17 Moon buggy was driven the furthest, over **21** miles.

$25.8 billion The cost of the whole Apollo program ($194.3 billion at today's prices).

The Moon's gravity is **1/6** of Earth's gravity.

Ganymede

3,273

The diameter in miles of the largest moon in the Solar System, Jupiter's moon Ganymede—it's bigger than the planet Mercury!

The Apollo missions brought back **842** pounds of Moon rock.

OUR PLANET

We live on Earth—a big, blue planet that travels through space. And we're not the only ones here—in fact it is full of life!

Animals and plants live on the land and in the oceans too!

Polar bear

Is there life on other planets?

Not that we know of. There are living things on Earth because there is air, water, warmth, and light.

It's night time where the Earth faces away from the Sun.

Penguin

South Pole

Why is it dark at night?

As the Earth travels around the Sun it spins, too. This means sunlight can only shine on one part of the Earth at a time.

Why does the Earth need the Sun?

The Sun is a giant, hot star in space, and the Earth travels around it. The Sun gives us just the right amount of light and heat for plants to grow. Without the Sun, the Earth would be a dark and frozen planet, and nothing could live.

Is Earth like a jigsaw?

Yes, because it's made of pieces that fit together! The pieces are called plates and they are made of rock. The thickest parts of the plates poke up above the sea to form dry land, where we live.

The plates float on hot rock

The plates are always moving very slowly and creating new land, seas, and mountains

How do mountains grow?

Mountains are the tallest parts of the planet. Most of them grow when one plate moves and crashes into another plate. The rocks bend and fold, making mountains.

When plates move they can create earthquakes and volcanoes.

How tall is the tallest mountain?

Mount Everest is the tallest mountain, and it is 29,032 feet high. Everest is part of a group of mountains called the Himalayas.

Bar-headed geese are some of the highest-flying birds. We can soar over the Himalayas.

Mountain goat

What lives on a mountain?

Nimble-footed snow leopards chase mountain goats across slippery slopes. Life is hard on a cold mountain because there is often snow all year round.

Snow leopard

Mountains are millions of years old, but some of the rocks deep inside the Rocky Mountains could have been made more than a billion years ago!

CRASH!

Moving plates smash together.

Hot rock

What is the water cycle?

The way that water moves around our planet is called the water cycle. Most of the world's water is salty.

Sun

Clouds start to form

Water vapor rises

Water is all around us, even when we can't see it. It's not just in the sea and rivers. It's also in the air and in the ground.

Salty water in the ocean warms up and turns into water vapor, a type of gas. This is called evaporation. The salt stays in the ocean.

People use fresh water to drink, cook, wash, grow their crops, and give to their animals.

How can a river power a town?

A river can power a town when it flows through a hydroelectric dam. The water passes through special machines that turn the river's energy into electricity.

What is the Equator?

The Equator is an imaginary line that cuts the Earth into two halves. Near the Equator, the weather is hot and sunny most of the time.

Arctic Circle

NORTH AMERICA

EUROPE

I am a jaguar, and I live in the tropical Amazon rain forest in South America.

The Sun shines strongly around the Equator, and there is daylight for 12 hours a day, every day.

Equator

SOUTH AMERICA

I am an emperor penguin and I live on frozen Antarctica with lots of other penguins, seals, and birds. This is the coldest place on Earth!

Where does the Sun shine at midnight?

During the summer months in the far north of the world, the Sun doesn't set. In places such as Canada, Alaska, Russia, Greenland, Norway, and Sweden the Sun can be seen in the sky at night. But in winter it is cold and dark all the time.

What is a rainy season?

Tropical places near the Equator are hot and humid. Strong winds called monsoons bring wet weather in summer. This is called the "rainy season."

Are all deserts hot?

No, a desert can be hot or cold, but it's a dry place because it rarely rains. More rain falls in the hot and sandy Sahara than in Antarctica, which is a frozen, windy desert that's covered in snow!

Hoodoos

Pillar

Arch

Why do desert rocks look so weird?

The wind picks up desert sand, and blasts it against the rock. Over time it carves out some amazing rock shapes such as hoodoos, pillars, and arches.

Why do I need such big ears?

Those big ears help a fennec fox lose excess heat in the Sahara. They're also good for listening out for burrowing bugs under the sand.

Why don't penguins get frostbite?

A penguin's body is suited to life at the Antarctic. Its thick feathers are like a waterproof blanket, and warm blood travels through the bird's feet so they don't freeze.

Penguins hold their eggs on their feet to keep them warm.

What's an oasis?

An oasis is a place where water can be found in a hot desert. It's one of the few places that plants can grow.

We're Bedouin people. We live in tents so we can take our homes with us when we travel to find an oasis, or food to eat.

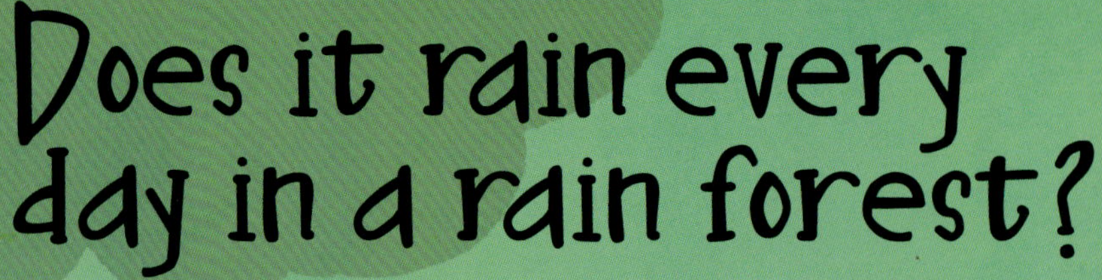

Does it rain every day in a rain forest?

It can! Rain forests are found in tropical areas around the Equator. The Amazon rain forest is the largest rain forest in the world. It's in South America and is home to millions of animals and plants, from tiny ants to giant trees.

Monkeys and parrots feast on the tropical fruits.

Why are plants important?

Animals need plants to survive because plants make oxygen. It's in the air, and we breathe it. Plants are also food for us and many other animals. When plants die they rot and turn into soil, which we use to grow more plants.

Rain forest plants have giant leaves and they grow flowers all year round.

The forest floor is home to fungi, frogs, and billions of ants and other bugs.

Trees grow tall and straight to reach the sunlight.
It can be noisy in a rain forest. Birds sing, insects buzz, and howler monkeys like me call and whoop to each other!
Lizards and snakes hunt insects.
Silent jaguars creep through the dark shadows or hide high up on branches.
Morpho butterfly
Lianas are climbing plants that have long, bendy stems and dangling branches.

What do we get from the Earth?

We get lots of things from the Earth! They are called natural resources. Animals and plants are used for food and clothing. We use metals and other minerals to make things. We can even use wind and water to give us power.

Plastics are strong and waterproof. They are often made from oil, which comes from the remains of tiny animals that once lived in the sea.

Glass is made from sand.

My bike is made of different materials that are found on Earth.

Rubber is a bendy, stretchy material that comes from rubber trees.

Rocks are made of different materials called minerals. Metals such as gold and silver are minerals. Most sand is a mineral called quartz.

Metal

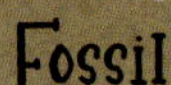

Where do diamonds come from?

Diamonds are a type of mineral that forms deep below the Earth's crust. Diamond is the hardest natural material, but it can be cut to make sparkly precious crystals or "stones."

What makes water wonderful?

Water is a liquid. It can freeze to become solid ice. It can turn into a gas called water vapor. Water may change its form, but it lasts forever.

2 It gets gassy

Heat from the Sun turns water into a gas, called water vapor. This is **evaporation**.

1 There's lots of it!

Over **two thirds** of the Earth's surface is covered in water.

Water is precious

Fresh water keeps us **alive**. Water helps plants grow, too. We can wash in it, swim in it, sail on it, and play in it!

3 It rises and cools

As warm water vapor rises, it cools down. It **condenses**, turning back into liquid.

4 It makes clouds

Water droplets or solid ice crystals gather around specks of dust and form **clouds**.

5 It falls back down

Water droplets or ice crystals form **raindrops** or **snowflakes**, which fall back to Earth.

6 It goes on and on

Rain and melted snow fill rivers, lakes, and oceans, then the whole **water cycle** starts all over again. It helps create our weather.

Where does the weather happen?

In the layer of the atmosphere that is closest to Earth's surface. The atmosphere surrounds our planet like a giant blanket, screening out some harmful rays that come from the Sun.

Atmosphere

Cumulonimbus

On TV, the weather is explained with maps and symbols.

What is a weather system?

Huge masses of air that swirl over Earth's surface are called weather systems. High pressure systems press air down against the land. They bring drier, clearer weather. Low pressure systems bring mild or rainy weather. The border between two systems is called a front.

Cirrus

Why do clouds have funny shapes?

Some clouds are white and puffy, some are thin and streaky. Some pile up like big dark towers, some form little blobs. Their shape depends on whether they are full of water droplets or ice crystals and how high up they are.

Some clouds look like dragons, castles, or bears in the sky. What can you see up there?

Mackerel sky

Is there a pot of gold at the end of a rainbow?

Only in fairy tales! Rainbows are the most beautiful sights in the sky. Air has no color, but when sunlight passes through rain or mist, the water droplets break up the light into an arc of shimmering colors.

Why does the wind blow?

Because as warm air rises, cold air whooshes in to take its place, and the wind blows! Some winds blow between land and sea. Some cross deserts and mountains. Others blow all the way around the planet.

How does the wind help plants?

Many trees and flowering plants have seeds that are scattered by the wind. Dandelion seeds are light and fluffy, and float a long way. Sycamore seeds are like helicopter blades, spinning around.

What is the monsoon?

It is a wind that blows across India. The winter monsoon brings dry weather. In summer it picks up lots of water from the ocean and brings heavy rains to the dry land.

Why do birds ride on the wind?

Wandering albatross

Condor

So we can fly long distances without too much flapping. Over the Southern Ocean, albatrosses like me glide on powerful winds. In South America, condors use currents of warm air to soar above mountains.

Pillar

How do winds shape rock?

Winds often carry dust, grit, or sand. They blast rocks and cliffs, wearing them down into all sorts of shapes. Water, ice, and heat also shape the surface of planet Earth.

What is a hurricane?

It's a terrifying tropical storm, also called a typhoon or a cyclone. A great storm cloud spins around as it sweeps over the ocean. Hurricane-force winds can reach 110 miles an hour or even more.

The calm center is called the "eye" of the storm.

Is it deadly?

When a hurricane smashes into land it can be deadly. There are huge waves, heavy rain, floods, and mudslides. Trees can be blown over, homes may be destroyed, and lives may be at risk.

Where is Tornado Alley?
This is an area in the United States that has some of the fiercest whirlwinds of all. They are called tornadoes or twisters. These dark funnels of dust can spin at up to 300 miles an hour. They can suck up a car or even a house.
WATCH OUT!
What is a waterspout?
A whirlwind that forms from warm, moist air over a sea or lake is called a waterspout. It is often joined to the bottom of a cloud.

Why are thunder clouds dark?

Thunder clouds are so full of water droplets that they look very dark. They tower up to 9 miles high.

How do clouds make lightning?

Water vapor rushes up into clouds from the warm ground. Once inside, the vapor cools and freezes, forming balls of ice called hailstones. Air currents ping these up and down inside the cloud, making an electric charge.

In a thunderstorm, stay away from water or metal fences.

BANG!
BOOM!
Thunderstorms can be dangerous.
Why does thunder go bang?
The heat of lightning is incredible, even hotter than the Sun. It makes the air expand so fast that it causes a shockwave. BANG!
How fast is lightning?
The electricity connects with the ground or with other clouds, forming a flash of lightning. This can travel 75,000 miles in a single second.
Which comes first, thunder or lightning?
They happen at the same time, but we see the flash first because light travels through the air faster than sound.
Go indoors if you can.
Do not stand under a tree.

How are snowflakes formed?

When water droplets freeze around specks of dust in a cloud, snowflakes form. These ice crystals freeze more droplets, building up amazing starry shapes and patterns. They stick together to make bigger flakes.

Snowflakes have SIX sides, or points.

What is a blizzard?

A blizzard is a heavy snow storm driven by high winds. Snow piles up in deep drifts. It's hard to see where you are going as everything looks white!

Why are mountaintops snowy?

Mountaintops are often covered in snow, even in hot countries. The higher you climb, the more the air expands and cools. This leads to more moisture—and snowy mountain conditions.

Where does frost make flowers?

Does the sea ever freeze?

Yes it does, but because the sea contains salt, it has a lower freezing point. It turns to ice below -35.6° Fahrenheit. Freshwater rivers and lakes freeze at 32° Fahrenheit.

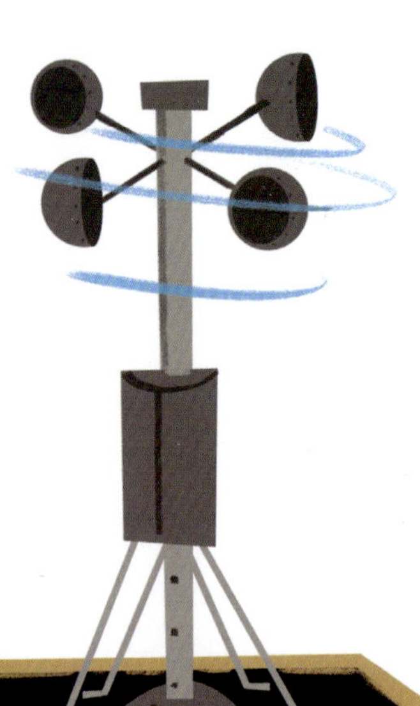

How do we measure the weather?

All sorts of clever gadgets have been invented over the years to measure how the weather behaves. Today, the numbers are often recorded and displayed digitally.

Anemometers measure wind speed. They are often fixed to tall buildings, bridges, and ships.

Rain gauges collect and measure the amount of rain that falls into a jar.

Thermometers measure how hot or cold it gets. The best known thermometers show how a liquid metal called mercury goes up or down inside a glass tube. Most weather scientists today use electrical resistance thermometers.

Barometers measure changes in air pressure. There are many different designs and displays.

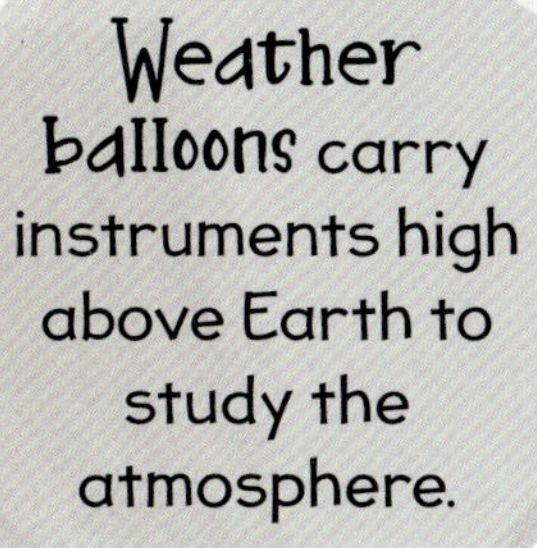

Weather balloons carry instruments high above Earth to study the atmosphere.

Satellites in space help us collect information about the climate. Buoys and ships at sea also record weather data, and so do aircraft.

Buoy

Weather science is called meteorology.

Did you know?

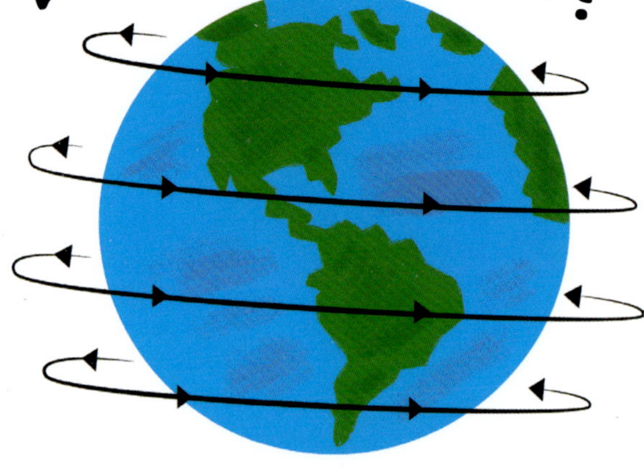

Super-powerful long-distance winds called **jet streams** rip along about 6.2 miles above the Earth's surface.

The Inuit people of the Arctic can build **igloos**—overnight shelters made from blocks of frozen snow. These are actually quite cozy!

Fog is just low-level cloud. The Grand Banks off Newfoundland, Canada, have about 206 foggy days each year.

It is said that no two **snowflakes** have exactly the same design!

As you are reading these words, there are about 2,000 **thunderstorms** happening around the world.

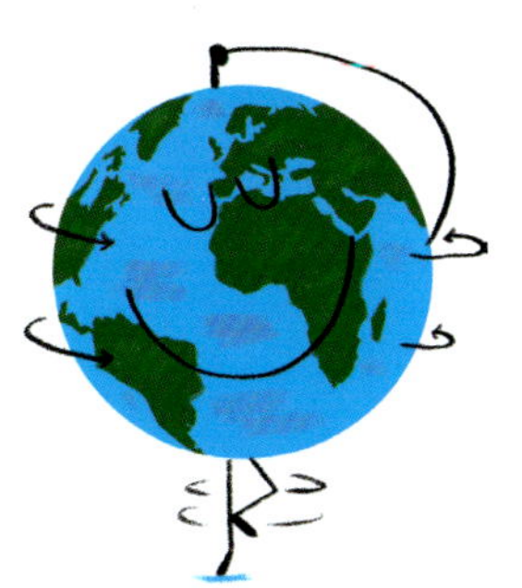

The spinning of the Earth forces **winds** that blow from the Poles to the Equator to change direction.

COUGH!

When fumes from cars and factories react with sunlight, the air is filled with horrible, poisonous **smog**.

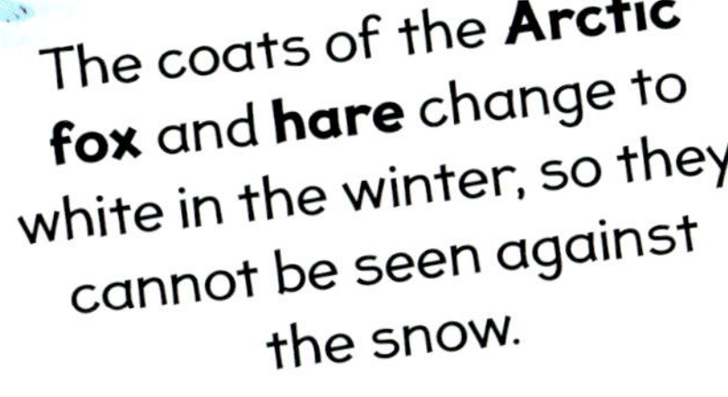

The coats of the **Arctic fox** and **hare** change to white in the winter, so they cannot be seen against the snow.

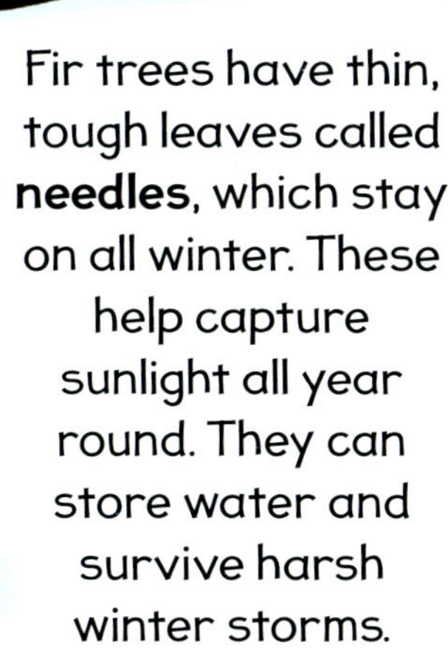

Fir trees have thin, tough leaves called **needles**, which stay on all winter. These help capture sunlight all year round. They can store water and survive harsh winter storms.

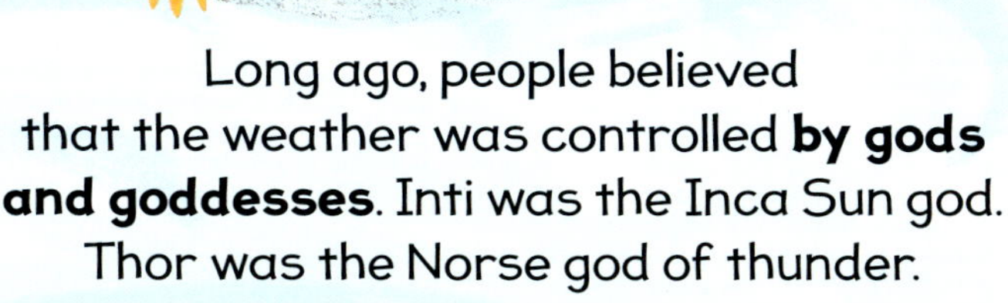

Long ago, people believed that the weather was controlled **by gods and goddesses**. Inti was the Inca Sun god. Thor was the Norse god of thunder.

OCEANS

Earth has five oceans and they are all HUGE! Together, they cover two thirds of Earth's surface.

NORTH AMERICA

ATLANTIC OCEAN

PACIFIC OCEAN

SOUTH AMERICA

Day octopus

SOUTHERN OCEAN

Seaweeds are plants that live in salty water.

Long-snouted seahorse

Are the oceans important?

Yes, billions of animals and plants live in them! People use the things that live in the ocean for all sorts of things, too. A type of seaweed called red algae is used in peanut butter—it makes it easy to spread!

Why is the sea blue?

Sunlight is made up of lots of colors. When it shines on the ocean, most of the colors disappear into the water, but blue light bounces back, so the ocean looks blue.

What is a fish?

Fish are animals that have skeletons, gills, and fins. There are more than 32,000 types, and most of them live in oceans.

Tail fin swishes from side to side when swimming.

Overlapping scales are smooth and slippery.

Herring

I'm the perfect shape for swimming. My silvery scales help water to flow easily over my skin.

Slim, sleek body moves quickly through water.

Can people breathe underwater too?

No—sorry! You need to breathe air because you have lungs. All fish have special organs called gills that work in water.

Water and air have oxygen gas in them. All animals need oxygen to live.

Oxygen-rich water flows in.

Triggerfish

Water flows out over the gills, where the oxygen passes into the fish's blood.

Do fish have special homes?

Some do. Clownfish live among the tentacles of stinging sea anemones. The fish are covered in special slime that protects them from stings, but animals that might want to eat them can't get close!

Can fish fly?

No—but some can glide. Flying fish have very streamlined bodies and use their big fins to launch out of the water into the air.

Who plays hide and seek?

Many ocean animals do! On coral reefs, millions of sea creatures live close together. Lots of them use clever tricks to avoid being eaten by the others.

Do fish need friends?

Can you see a reef from space?

Yes! The Great Barrier Reef stretches over 1,200 miles off the coast of Australia. Reefs are built by tiny animals called polyps. Each one lives in its own rocky cup, waving its tentacles in the water.

Who sleeps in a muddy bed?

Sea cucumbers do! These sluglike animals live in mud, eat mud, and poo mud! Sea cucumbers are animals, not vegetables, but some people do like to eat them!

The bottom of the sea is covered in mud and sand. It's called the seabed!

I'm a longnose sawshark. I hunt fish and crabs that are hiding in the mud. My nose is lined with sharp teeth!

I'm a glowing jellyfish called a mauve stinger.

How do people explore under the sea?

People can't breathe in water, but we still find ways to explore the deep ocean. We can scuba dive, use submarines, or send robots with cameras.

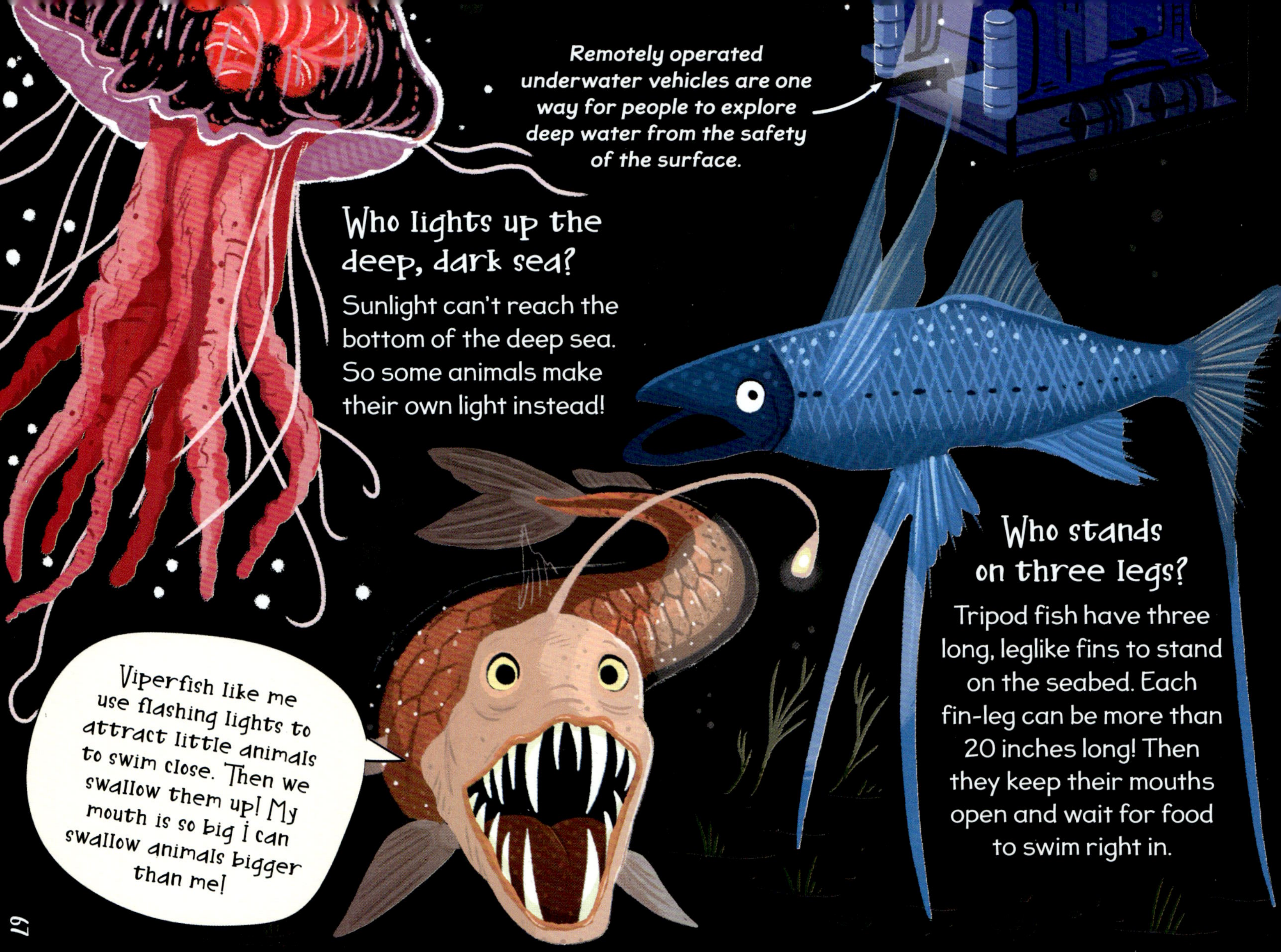

Remotely operated underwater vehicles are one way for people to explore deep water from the safety of the surface.

Who lights up the deep, dark sea?

Sunlight can't reach the bottom of the deep sea. So some animals make their own light instead!

Who stands on three legs?

Tripod fish have three long, leglike fins to stand on the seabed. Each fin-leg can be more than 20 inches long! Then they keep their mouths open and wait for food to swim right in.

Why does the sea go in and out?

Over the course of a day at the seaside you will see the sea moving in and out. This is called the tide, and it's caused by the Moon!

Who loves to surf?

Humans—but dolphins ride the waves too! Flat water turns to waves when wind blows over the top of it.

Which animals go to school?

Who snacks at the shore?

Gray seals feed on all kinds of animals near the shore, from crabs to seabirds. They can also dive to depths of 230 feet when hunting.

Are there monsters in the sea?

There are some very big animals in the sea... but no monsters. From huge rays and outsize crabs to the biggest animal on Earth—plenty of giants lurk in the deep.

Why do whales spout water?

That's how they breathe! Whales breathe air. They all have one or two blowholes, which are like nostrils. A spout from a whale is really just a big, warm, wet breath!

Which crab has the longest legs?

A Japanese spider crab has 10 legs, and each leg can be over 6.5 feet long! These mega crabs can reach 100 years old.

What's the biggest animal?

Me! I'm also the biggest animal to ever live! I can grow up to 82 feet long and my tongue weighs the same as an elephant.

Could you sink a ship?
Giant manta ray
No! Sailors used to think fish like me could pull a ship under the water. They even called me devil fish! It wasn't true—I'm huge (up to 23 feet wide) but harmless.
Blue whale
Giant octopus
Who can reach you from 13 feet away?
Me! My eight arms are each 13 feet long, with more than 200 strong suckers on each one.

A compendium of questions

Can I drink seawater?

No—it can make you sick. Seawater is too salty, and often dirty too. The dirt is called pollution and it's bad for all living things.

Can I swim across an ocean?

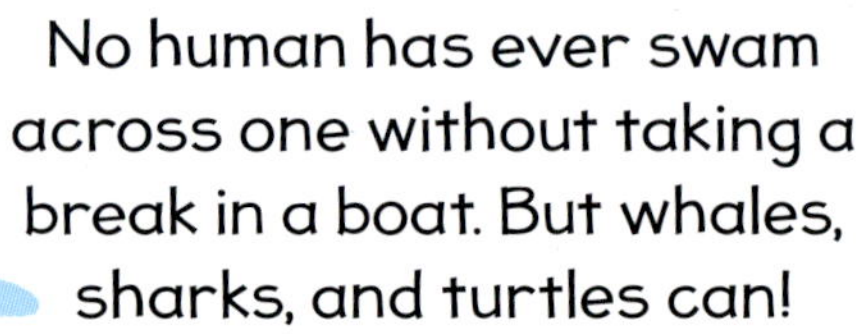

No human has ever swam across one without taking a break in a boat. But whales, sharks, and turtles can!

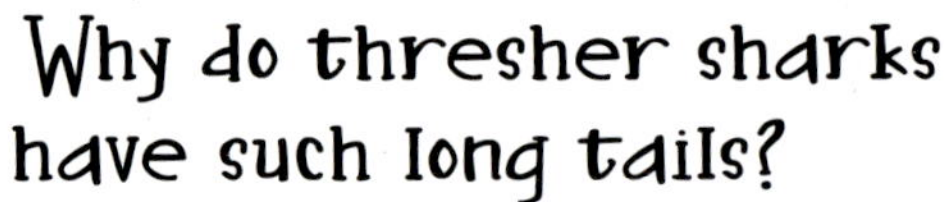

Why do thresher sharks have such long tails?

They use the enormous upper lobes of their tail fins to wallop shoals of their fish prey.

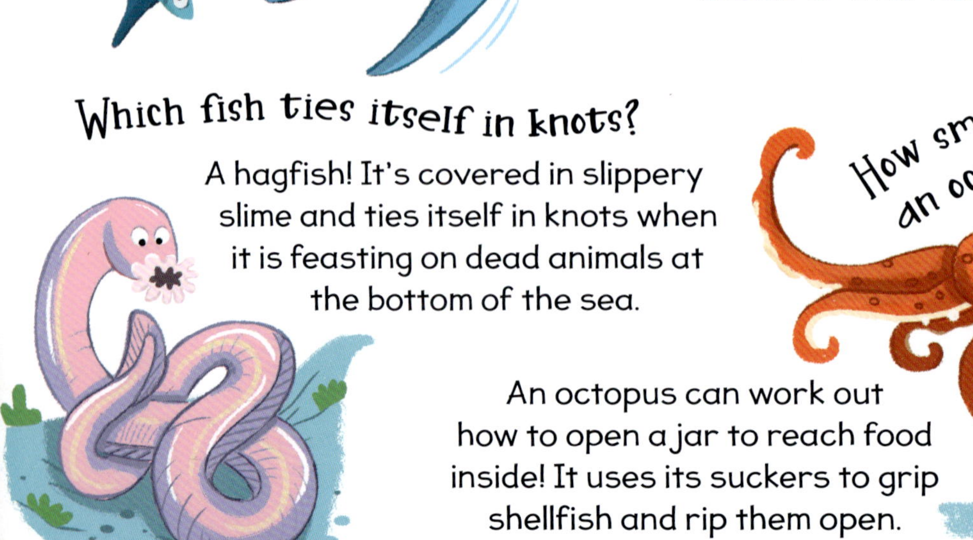

Which fish ties itself in knots?

A hagfish! It's covered in slippery slime and ties itself in knots when it is feasting on dead animals at the bottom of the sea.

How smart is an octopus?

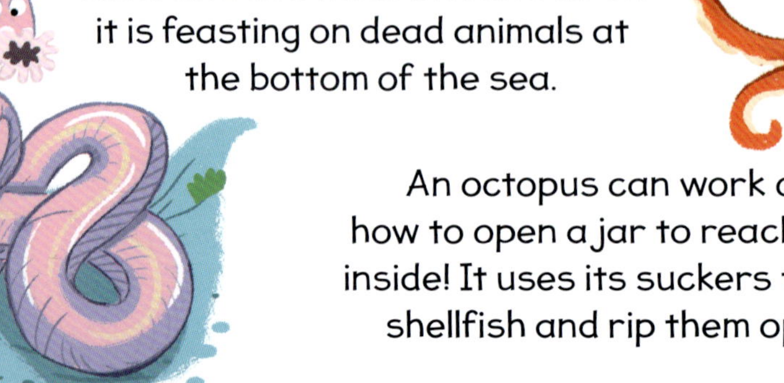

An octopus can work out how to open a jar to reach food inside! It uses its suckers to grip shellfish and rip them open.

Why is a blobfish so ugly?

I'm prettier underwater!

When a blobfish is brought to the surface of the sea its soft, spongy flesh goes floppy. When it is busy hunting in the deep sea it looks quite different.

Why does a firefly squid glow?

To hide, and to be seen! This squid can mimic the light above or below it if it wants to hide, and glow brightly when it wants to attract a mate.

Did that fish's eye just move?

Maybe! Baby flounders have an eye on each side of their head. As they grow, one eye moves to join the other—so the adult flounder can spend its days lying on the seafloor.

Which fish uses oars?

The fins of the strange, ribbonlike oarfish look a bit like oars. It's the longest bony fish—reaching up to 36 feet.

PLANTS

A plant is a living thing that can...

① Make new plants

Plants may not have babies but they can make new plants that look just like them! It's called **reproduction** and most plants do this by making seeds.

Leaves

Stem

Seed

Seeds grow into new plants, which then make more seeds.

② Breathe

Plants **breathe** air through tiny holes in their leaves.

③ Get rid of waste

Plants are brilliant because when they breathe they make a **waste** gas called oxygen—it's the gas we need to stay alive!

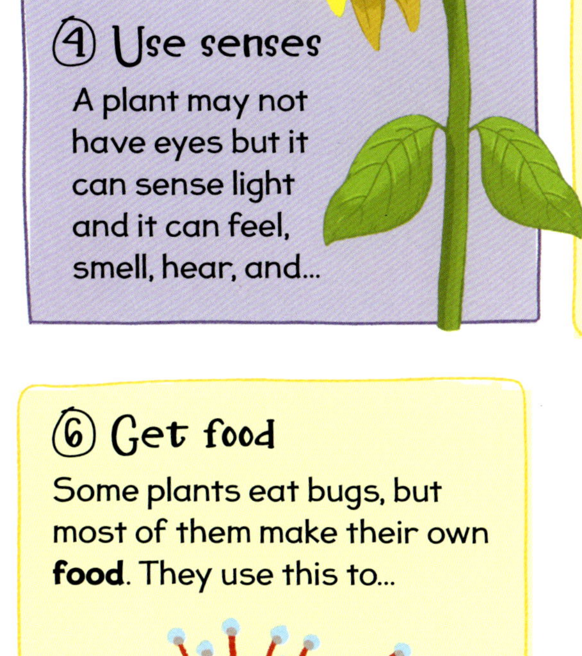

④ Use senses

A plant may not have eyes but it can sense light and it can feel, smell, hear, and...

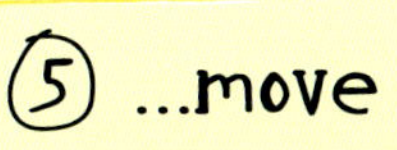

⑤ ...move

Plants **move** their leaves to face the Sun. Seeds **travel** too. Some of them are carried a long way on the wind.

⑥ Get food

Some plants eat bugs, but most of them make their own **food**. They use this to...

⑦ ...grow

Most plants—even giant trees—start their lives as seeds, but they soon grow and change.

Do plants get hungry?

Plants don't feel hungry the same way that animals do, but they do need food. Animals eat their food, but plants make all the food they need.

Sunlight

Flowering plant

I can store the food I make in different parts of me and save it for the winter.

Flower

Leaf

Stem

Oxygen out

Carbon dioxide in

Plants use sunlight to turn water and carbon dioxide from the air into food. This is called photosynthesis.

Why are leaves green?

Because they have a green substance called chlorophyll inside them. This helps the plant collect the energy from sunlight and turn it into food.

Water is sucked up from the soil by a plant's roots.

Roots also suck up minerals to help a plant grow.

How do plants feed the world?

Plants are the beginning of most food chains. This is when living things depend on each other for food. Animals eat plants—fruits, vegetables, nuts, and seeds—and some animals also eat other animals.

A food chain shows how energy and nutrients pass from one living thing to another.

Why do plants lose their leaves?

In the fall many leaves change color and fall off. This is so the plant can store up water and energy over the winter, ready to grow new leaves in the spring.

Which plants snap, munch, and stick?

Some plants don't just make food from sunlight. They eat things too! They are called carnivorous, or meat-eating, plants.

How do plants catch bugs?

Venus flytraps have trap-shaped leaves coated in hairs. When a spider, beetle, or fly crawls over the hairs, the plant's trap snaps shut! The bug tries to escape, but there is no way out.

Which plants drown their food?

Pitcher plants grow jug-shaped leaves that fill with water. Small creatures are tempted by the plant's smell and fall in, often drowning in the liquid at the bottom of the "jug."

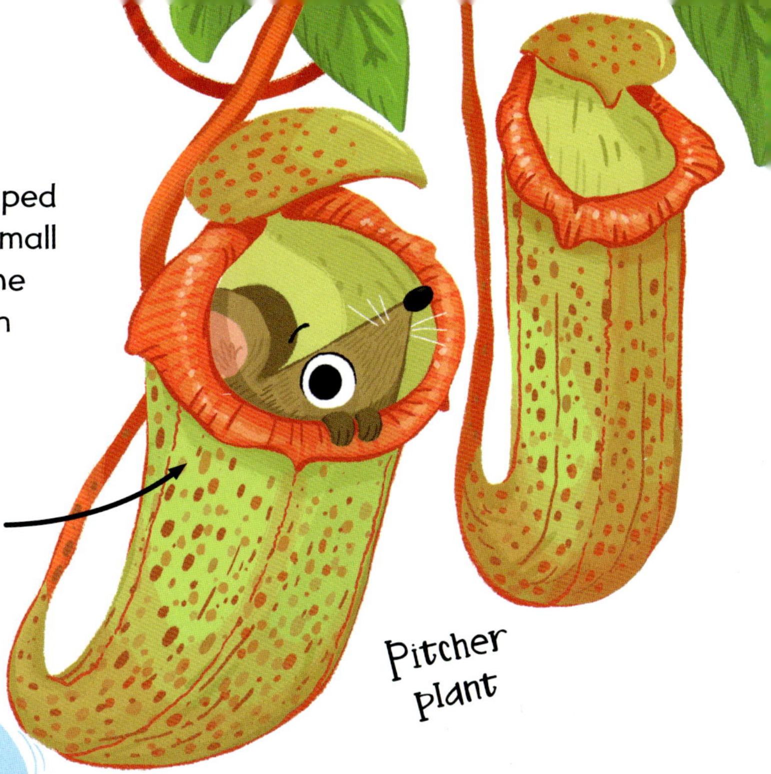

Some pitcher plants are big enough to catch frogs and mice!

Stick!

Pitcher plant

Which plants trap with glue?

Sundew plant

Sundew plants have delicious-looking red droplets that attract passing bugs. They are actually sticky glue, and when a bug lands on them it sticks. The plant then folds over and begins to dissolve the bug. Yum!

Once I trap my prey, I make liquid that dissolves the bug into a gloopy soup.

Why are flowers pretty?

Flowers have a very important job to do—it's called pollination—and many of them need insects to help. Colors, smells, and shapes of flowers attract insects to a plant to pollinate it.

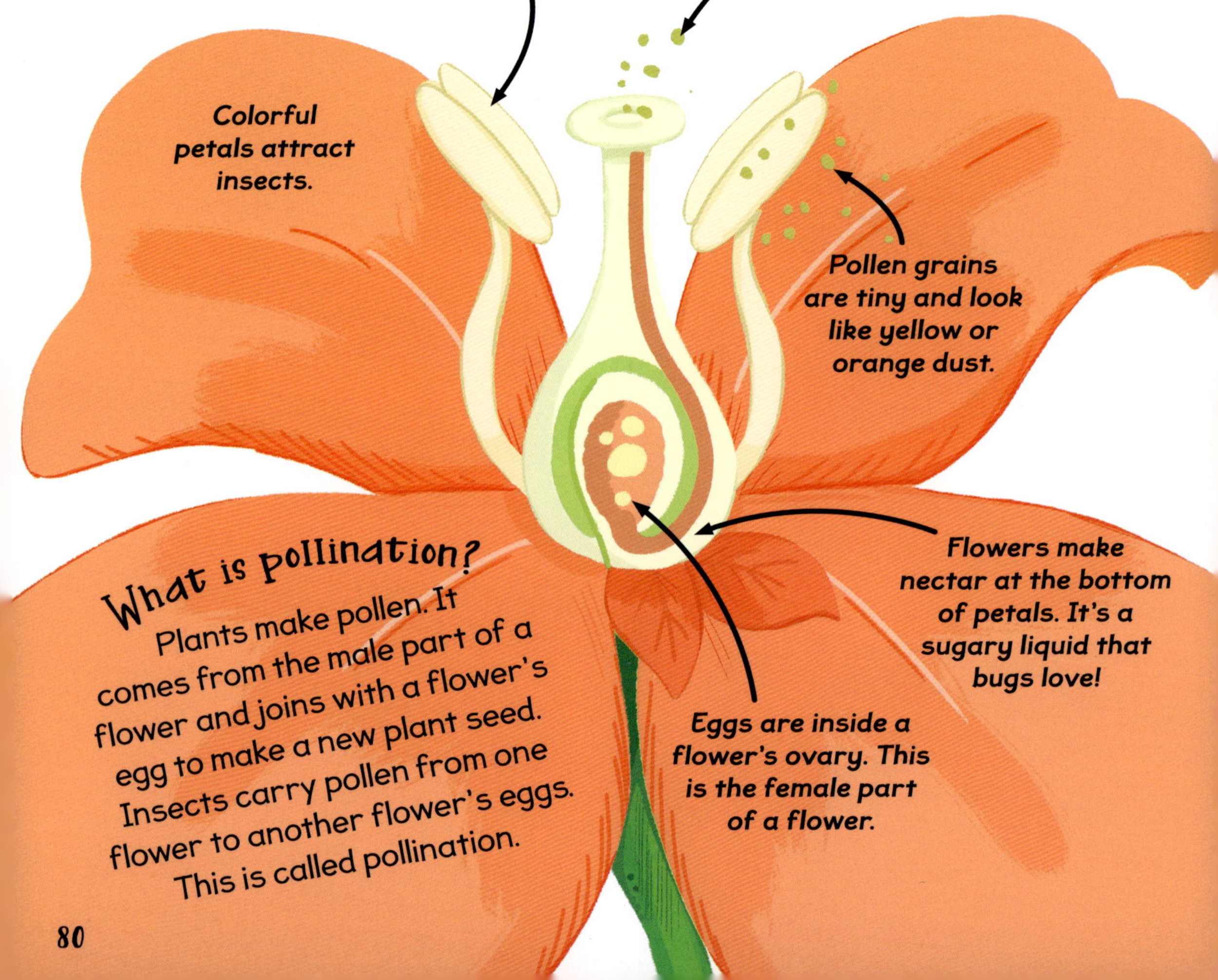

Pollen grows on stamens—the male parts of a flower.

Pollen lands here and grows a tube down to the ovary to make new seeds.

Colorful petals attract insects.

Pollen grains are tiny and look like yellow or orange dust.

Flowers make nectar at the bottom of petals. It's a sugary liquid that bugs love!

Eggs are inside a flower's ovary. This is the female part of a flower.

What is pollination?

Plants make pollen. It comes from the male part of a flower and joins with a flower's egg to make a new plant seed. Insects carry pollen from one flower to another flower's eggs. This is called pollination.

Why do bees have baskets?

Some bees have special pouches on their legs that they use as baskets to carry the pollen they collect from flowers.

Why do bananas need bats?

Banana, cocoa, and mango plants are pollinated by bats. They visit the flowers to drink nectar, get covered in pollen, and carry it from plant to plant. Birds and moths also pollinate some plants.

Why are tomatoes red?

Tomatoes and other fruits are colorful to tell animals that they are ripe and ready to eat.

I'm tiny and green because I'm not ready to eat!

Fruits have seeds in them. When animals eat the fruits, and then poop, they spread the seeds to new places where they grow into new plants.

I'm red, plump, juicy, and sweet. Eat me!

Tomato plant

Apple

Seeds

Warning!

Only eat fruits and nuts you have been told are safe to eat.

Why do fruits grow?

When a plant grows some new seeds, the fruit of the plant grows around the seeds to protect them.

Can seeds grow inside me?

Seeds can't grow inside animals or people. They need soil, water, and oxygen to start growing.

Water goes into the seed and it swells.

There is food in the seed for the new plant.

Why are nuts hard?

Nuts are hard fruits. They are hard to protect the seeds inside, or to help them move safely to new places.

How do plants stay safe?

Many animals eat plants, and that's not good news for our green friends! They need to defend themselves from attack and some use prickly thorns and poisons to do this.

Who hugs trees to death?

Warning!

Only eat berries you have been told are safe to eat.

Why are some berries deadly?

Berries often look tasty, but some contain poison to put animals off eating them. Deadly nightshade and foxglove plants can stop your heart from beating, but doctors can also make medicines from them.

What's the point of thorns and prickles?

Many plants have sharp thorns and prickles to stop animals from eating them.

Why do nettles sting?

Nettles have tiny stinging hairs, each with a bead of acid on its tip. If you touch a nettle the hairs prick your skin and the beads release the acid.

How big is the tallest tree?

The tallest tree is a coast redwood called Hyperion in California, U.S., and it's taller than a 27-story building! It is about 380 feet tall, and it grows 1.6 inches taller every year. How much have you grown in the past year?

I have more than 550 million leaves!

Why do people hug trees?

You can hug a tree to work out how big and how old it is. As trees age they get taller but their trunks also get wider. If it takes six children or more to hug an oak tree then it's very old.

Coast redwood

Is a mushroom a plant?

No, mushrooms are a type of fungus but, like plants and animals, they are alive. They can grow on dead trees using the wood as their food.

What's that knocking sound?

It's a deathwatch beetle inside rotting wood tapping to attract a mate! In the forest, dead trees and logs make a great place for insects to live and start a family.

How many?

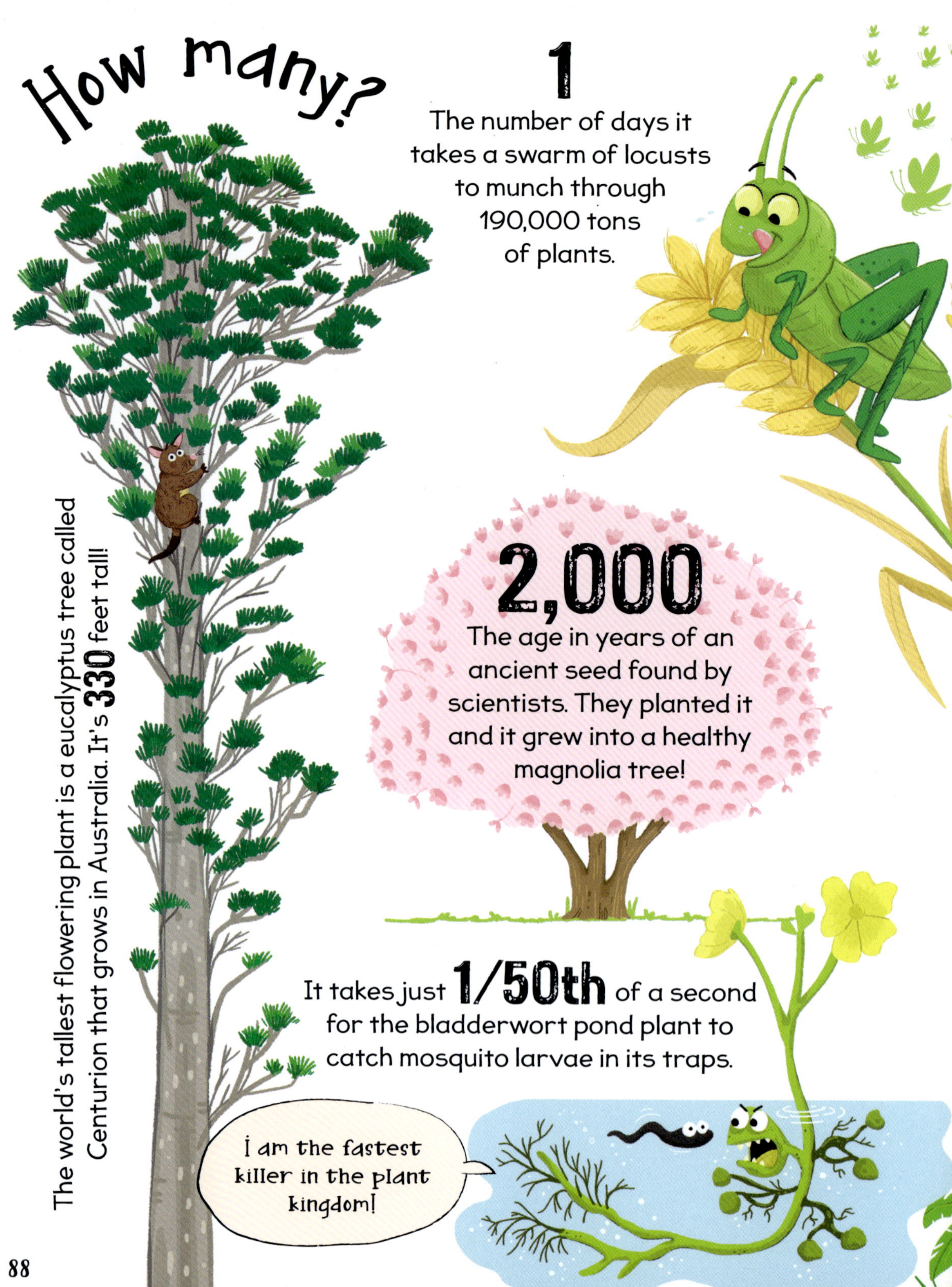

1

The number of days it takes a swarm of locusts to munch through 190,000 tons of plants.

2,000

The age in years of an ancient seed found by scientists. They planted it and it grew into a healthy magnolia tree!

It takes just **1/50th** of a second for the bladderwort pond plant to catch mosquito larvae in its traps.

The world's tallest flowering plant is a eucalyptus tree called Centurion that grows in Australia. It's **330** feet tall!

150 years old—the age of a giant bromeliad before it grows its first flower. It dies afterward.

It can take **10** days for a Venus flytrap to digest a dead bug.

A saguaro cactus grows just **2** inches in ten years, but bamboo can grow **14** inches in a single day!

43

The number of gallons of water one corn plant needs to grow. That's more than two full bathtubs!

500 different types of plant are pollinated by bats.

There are **12,500** different types of tree growing in the Amazon rain forest.

DINOSAURS

The first dinosaurs lived about 240 million years ago, long before there were people. Dinosaurs evolved from other animals called dinosauromorphs. They were cat-sized reptiles.

Were all dinosaurs huge?

Dinosaurs came in all shapes and sizes. The largest ones were called titanosaurs. They were more than 65 feet long and weighed as much as six elephants!

Argentinosaurus

I'm one of the biggest dinosaurs ever. Can you guess where in the world I came from?

This tiny terror is Microraptor. It is just 15–23 inches long.

Being small helps me to glide from trees.

Where did they live?

The first dinosaurs lived on Pangaea—a single, giant slab of land. The world was very hot and dry and there was just one ocean called Panthalassa. Dinosaurs could walk all the way from the North Pole to the South Pole. We call this time in Earth's history the Triassic.

Which dinosaurs had the longest necks?

Sauropods were a group of huge dinosaurs with very long necks, like *Brachiosaurus*. Having a long neck meant that sauropods could reach high up into trees to eat leaves. They might spend all day eating.

Mamenchisaurus had a long, thin neck that was 39 feet in length.

Mamenchisaurus

Brachiosaurus

Parasaurolophus

Could dinosaurs roaaarr?

No one knows what sounds dinosaurs made. They may have roared, growled, chirped, tweeted—or made no sounds at all. *Parasaurolophus* had a long, hollow crest on its head. It may have blown air through the crest to make honking sounds—like a trumpet!

Diplodocus had a long, bendy tail too, which it used to wallop other dinosaurs.

Some dinosaurs liked to look good! Horns, frills, head plates, and colorful feathers or skin may have all helped male dinosaurs look attractive to female ones.

Who was king of the dinosaurs?

Look out! Here comes *Tyrannosaurus rex*—king of the dinosaurs. *T-Rex* was a massive 42 feet long and weighed about 7.7 tons—that makes it one of the biggest meat-eaters that's ever lived on land, in the whole history of the planet!

How scary was a T-Rex?

T-Rex was one of the scariest dinosaurs to ever live. It was a huge, fearsome, powerful hunter that preyed on other big dinosaurs. It could bite its prey so hard it snapped bones.

When did T-Rex live?

T-Rex lived at the end of the Cretaceous Period, 68 to 66 million years ago. Scientists have so far found about 50 skeletons of *T-Rex* in North America.

T-Rex had small arms and hands but they were very strong, and had nasty claws. *T-Rex* may have gripped prey close to its chest as it sank its razor-sharp teeth into the flesh.

How did dinosaurs defend themselves?

Many plant-eating dinosaurs had bony armor to protect them from attack. Thick slabs of bone, plates, scales, spikes, and bony bumps all helped ankylosaurs fend off the razor-sharp claws and daggerlike teeth of meat-eating dinosaurs.

T-Rex
Why did Triceratops have horns?
Roar!
I use my long horns to defend myself against T-Rex and other big predators. I can raise the big bony frill around my neck to make myself look scarier too!
I'm a bonehead dinosaur. My skull is 10 inches thick. I can use it to batter my rivals, and it makes me look cool too!
Why is your head so big?
Bonehead dinosaurs used their big heads to ram into each other.
Pachycephalosaurus
Crash!

What did dinosaurs eat?

Some dinosaurs hunted animals to eat, other dinosaurs ate plants, and some ate whatever they could find!

I'm fully armed with slashing, gripping claws and jaws lined with razor-sharp teeth. I'm fast, smart... and hungry for meat!

Saurpelta

Raptors, like Deinonychus, were light on their feet and super speedy.

I eat plants. My body is covered in bony plates and spikes that make it difficult for Deinonychus to attack me!

How much did T-Rex eat?

Yum!

T-Rex was a hungry beast that needed about 240 pounds of meat a day. That's more than 1,000 burgers!

How fast could a dinosaur run?

Plant-eating dinosaurs were slow movers, but most predator dinosaurs needed speed to hunt and catch their prey.

***Ornithomimus** was one of the fastest dinosaurs, with top speeds of 31 miles an hour or more.*

Could dinosaurs fly?

Yes, and they still do! Flying dinosaurs are all around us. We call them birds.

Over a long time, some dinosaurs began to develop birdlike bodies with wings and feathers. By 150 million years ago, the first birds had appeared. That means all birds are actually dinosaurs!

What was the first bird called?

Archaeopteryx—that's me! I have teeth, claws on my wings, and a long, bony tail. I can climb, run, glide, and even fly a little.

What is a pterosaur?

Pterosaurs were flying reptiles that lived at the same time as the dinosaurs. Their wings were made of thin skin, spread out between the bones in their arms and fingers, and they were superb flyers.

How could sauropods grow so big?

Sauropods were giant plant-eaters. They had big bones and huge muscles to move their bodies. They also had holes and air sacs in their bones, which kept them light. Without these, sauropods would have been even heavier!

Could a dinosaur crush a car?

Argentinosaurus weighed over 66 tons. If it sat on a car, it could crush it in an instant! *T-Rex* had one of the most powerful bites of any animal ever known. It could have crushed a car in its mighty jaws!

How did dinosaurs kill their prey?

They were equipped with some lethal weapons! Claws, jaws, teeth, and tails could all be used to injure, catch, or kill other animals. Raptors had long, curved claws on their feet for slashing and slicing.

What happened to the dinosaurs?

After more than 150 million years of ruling the world, disaster struck the dinosaurs. An enormous space rock, called an asteroid, smashed into Earth.

How did Earth change?

It turned cold and dark, and there was very little food because plants couldn't grow. Over the next few thousand years, most types of animals, including the dinosaurs, went extinct.

The dinosaurs began to die, along with many other animals.

Are the dinosaurs still alive?

Yes they are! Birds belong to the dinosaur family, and some survived the asteroid, along with other animals. Today, more than 10,000 different types of bird live all over the world.

Eagles have sharp claws and beaks like many dinosaurs did.

Huge, flightless terror birds lived in South America about two million years ago.

Ducks, geese, and chickens are dinosaur relatives.

A compendium of questions

What was the biggest scary dinosaur to ever live?

It may have been the super scary *Spinosaurus*. It was probably longer and heavier than *T-Rex*, and its huge head had crocodile-like jaws lined with teeth.

How many types of dinosaur are there?

About 2,000 types have been found and named so far, but there are plenty more to discover.

Why did Brachiosaurus eat stones?

Like many reptiles, *Brachiosaurus* probably swallowed stones to help grind up tough plant food in its stomach.

Were dinosaurs clever?

Some were! *Troodon* had a big brain for its size. It was smarter than a turtle, but not as clever as a parrot.

Could I out-run a Velociraptor?

No! *Velociraptor* could reach speeds of 21 miles an hour. Few animals could escape those razor-sharp claws!

Were pterosaurs flying dinosaurs?

Pterosaurs could fly, but they were not dinosaurs. They belonged to a group of reptiles that appeared before the first dinosaurs.

Which dino could fish?

Deinocheirus could. It had very long arms and sharp claws. It may have reached into rivers to grab fish or reached high into trees to pick fruit.

Which dinosaur loved stinky smells?

Tarbosaurus was a hunter, but also ate dead animals that it found by following the stench of rotting flesh.

Were any dinosaurs friendly?

Some dinosaurs, like *Iguanodon*, probably lived peacefully in herds. *T-Rex* might have hunted in packs, but was probably not friendly!

ANIMALS

How do we know what an animal is? Animals are living things that do all of these things...

① Have babies

All animals can make new life like themselves—this is called **having babies**, or **reproduction**.

② Breathe

Animals **breathe** to take air into their bodies. The body needs a gas in the air called oxygen to keep working.

③ Use senses

An animal uses the **senses** of touch, taste, smell, sight, and hearing to find out what is going on around it.

④ Move

Most animals **move** to get to food and water, to find safe places, and to escape from danger.

I learned to stand up 30 minutes after I was born. How old were you when you learned to stand?

⑤ Eat

Animals must **eat** food to stay alive. Food gives them energy so they can **move** and **grow**.

Munch!

⑥ Get rid of waste

Waste is leftover food that an animal's body doesn't need.

Waste not want not! Dung beetles like me use elephant poo for lots of things!

⑦ Grow

All animals start small and **grow** bigger until they are old enough to **have babies** of their own.

What are senses?

Senses are the body's way of finding out about the world. Animals use senses to locate food, find their way around, avoid danger, and make friends. The five main senses are **hearing**, **sight**, **smell**, **taste**, and **touch**.

HEARING

Ear

Do bugs have ears?

Yes—lots of bugs can hear better than humans, but our ears can be in strange places! I'm a bush cricket, and my ears are on my legs.

TOUCH

What are whiskers for?

A cat's whiskers are super-sensitive. I use them to feel things—they can tell me if a space I want to crawl into is too small for my body.

How do snakes smell?
Snakes can smell with their tongues. They flick them in the air to detect any appealing odors!
SMELL
TASTE
Why is it a bad idea to lick a frog?
I make a foul-tasting slime in my skin. It stops animals from eating me.
SIGHT
Do all animals have two eyes?
Some animals have more than two! Most spiders have eight eyes, but cave spiders have none. They live in caves where it's always dark.

What's inside an animal?

If you had to build an animal from scratch, here's what you would need...

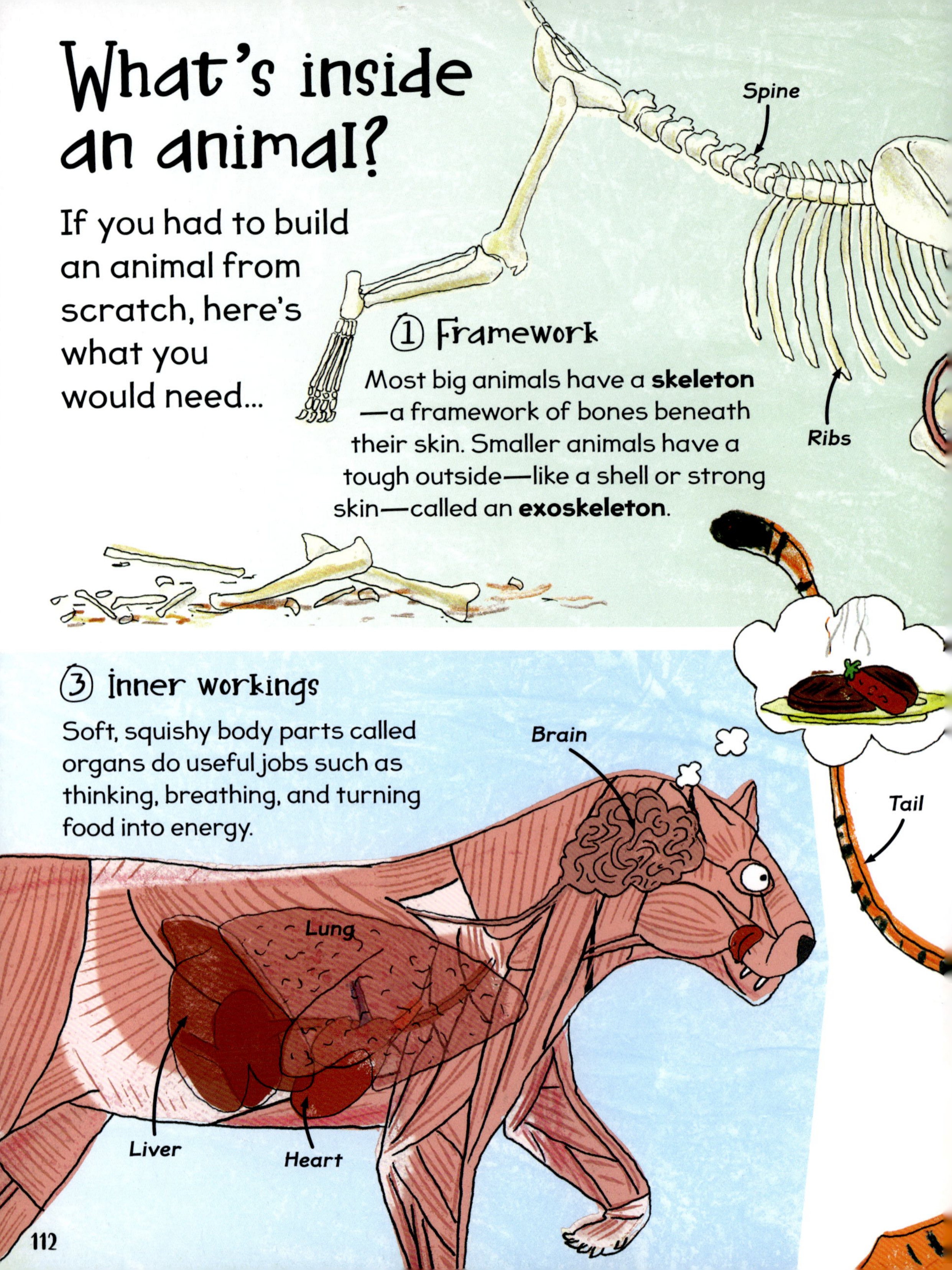

① Framework

Most big animals have a **skeleton**—a framework of bones beneath their skin. Smaller animals have a tough outside—like a shell or strong skin—called an **exoskeleton**.

③ Inner workings

Soft, squishy body parts called organs do useful jobs such as thinking, breathing, and turning food into energy.

② Power

Animals need muscles to move—even wriggly worms have muscles! A tiger uses hundreds of muscles to run, climb, or jump.

④ Special effects

Some animals have fur, some feathers, and some have scales. Tigers have striped fur to help them hide in tall grass. Why do you think they have sharp teeth and claws?

Why are you blue?

Colors and patterns make an animal beautiful! They can also make an animal look scary, or help it to hide.

Blue-ringed octopus

My color is a sign of danger. When I'm scared, blue circles appear on my skin. They are a warning that I can kill any attackers with venom.

Blue morpho butterfly

Danger or disguise?

Some animals blend into the background. This is called camouflage. Others have colors and patterns that warn enemies to stay away. Which of these creatures are using camouflage, and which are using warning colors?

Strawberry poison dart frog

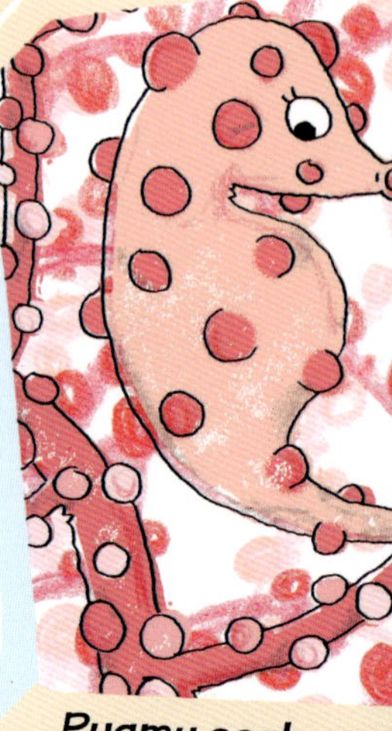

Pygmy seahorse

My colors help me hide. A blue or dark gray shark can prowl through the sea, unseen by the fish it is looking for.
Blue shark
Would you rather have blue feet, like me, or a blue bum, like a baboon?
Southern crowned-pigeon
Blue-footed booby
My beautiful blue feathers make me look healthy and fit to attract a mate.
Banded sea krait
Lion
Leaf insect

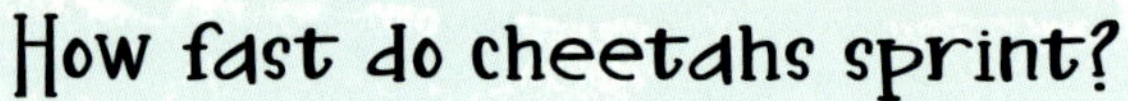

How fast do cheetahs sprint?

A cheetah is the fastest running animal on the planet. It can reach top speeds of up to 60 miles per hour.

① Built for speed

A cheetah's body is packed with small, but powerful muscles.

Why do cheetahs run fast?

Like many hunters, cheetahs turn on the speed when they want to catch their lunch! The antelope they chase need to be fast too, if they hope to escape.

Why are tortoises so slow?

Tortoises plod along slowly because they don't need speed to catch their lunch—they eat grass! They don't need to be fast to escape from danger either because their tough shells protect them like a suit of armor.

② Big strides

It has a super-bendy spine and long, slim legs.

③ Long leap

All four of a cheetah's feet leave the ground as it runs.

Why do crabs run sideways?

Because the way their legs bend means they can't run forward!

Who's playing statues?

During the day, a potoo bird doesn't move at all! It pretends to be a branch. At night, it flies about, hunting bugs to eat.

Is anyone at home?

Yes! An animal's home is a safe place where it can look after its babies. Animal homes are called habitats. They can be as big as an ocean or as small as a single leaf.

Froghopper nest.

Who lives in a home made of spit?

Young froghopper insects build a home of froth around themselves! This "spit" keeps them safe while they grow.

Why do frogs like water?

Because they need to lay their eggs in it. They are amphibians, which means they can live in water or on land.

Some animals that live in or near water have to come up to the surface to breathe air.

Others have gills and breathe underwater.

Frogs like to live in wet places.

Birds nest in tree branches.
Owls and their chicks live in tree holes.
Why do owls hoot?
They hoot to tell other owls to stay away from their tree. Some animals don't like neighbors!
This fox den is under the tree's roots.
Ladybugs also lay their eggs on leaves.
Would you rather live in a treetop nest with chicks, or in an underground sett with badger cubs?

Did you know?
A **fulmar** is a foul seabird. It spits a stinky oil at anyone who gets too close.
The **giraffe** is the tallest animal that lives on land.
Lobsters have blue blood and some dogs have blue tongues.
When a **sandtiger shark** wants to sink to the seabed, it has to burp first!
A spiny **sea urchin** is covered in tiny feet. Its mouth is on its bottom!
Mimic octopuses can change shape and color. They can pretend to be fish or sea snakes.
Sweat bees like the smell and taste of human sweat!
If a **sponge** is broken into bits, this strange sea creature is able to put itself back together again.

The **dung beetle** is the strongest animal on Earth. If it were the size of a human it could pull six buses full of people!

A **spider** eats about 2,000 bugs a year.

Australian **burrowing frogs** cover themselves in slime, so when flies land on them they get stuck—and the frogs can gobble them up.

Bees waggle their bottoms in a crazy dance to tell each other where to find the best flowers.

Hippos don't just yawn when they are tired—they also yawn when they are angry or scared.

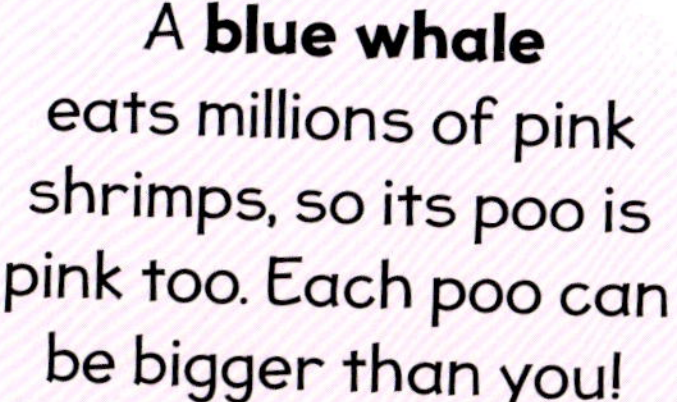

A **blue whale** eats millions of pink shrimps, so its poo is pink too. Each poo can be bigger than you!

A **catfish** can use its whole body to taste. Its skin is covered with taste buds.

MY BODY

Your body lets you see, hear, smell, taste, and touch the world around you. You can use it to run, jump, think, talk, and have all kinds of fun. Without it, you couldn't do anything.

Our bodies look different on the outside, but inside we all have bones, muscles, and blood.

Cells make up tissue such as bone, muscle, and blood.

Why are cells so special?

Because they are the tiny building blocks that together make up your body. Different cells do different jobs. You have blood cells, bone cells, skin cells, and lots more.

Bone cells make up your skeleton.

How can doctors see inside our bodies?

Doctors can look inside the body with scans and X-rays to see where all the parts are and how they fit together. They can even look at single cells with microscopes that magnify them.

Muscle cells help to form every muscle in your body.

Your blood contains trillions of red blood cells.

Why do I need to eat?

Food provides the energy your body needs to keep working. Chemicals from food repair your body and help it grow. Your body breaks down food and rearranges the chemicals to make skin, hair, bones, and all the other parts.

Can I balance my food?

Yes you can, but not on your head! It's important to eat a wide range of foods from different food groups to make sure you stay fit and healthy.

Why is water so important?

About 60 percent of your body is water—it's in every cell. But you lose water when you pee and sweat, and every time you breathe out. You need to drink to replace the water you lose.

What happens when I eat?

The food you eat takes a long and twisty route through your digestive system. At each stage, your body pulls out the good things it needs.

1 How do teeth help?

Your teeth break up food as you chew. They chew it into smaller pieces and mash it around. Food mixes with saliva in your mouth, making it easier to swallow.

2 Where does food go first?

When you swallow, food goes into a tube in your throat called your esophagus (say "ee-sof-a-guss"). Muscles push the food down to your stomach, squeezing behind the lump of food so that it moves along.

③ Why is there acid in my stomach?

Acid dissolves food into a gloopy liquid. Muscles in your stomach also churn the mixture around to break it up.

④ What goes on in my intestines?

A milky mushy liquid moves into and through your intestines where nutrients (useful chemicals) and water are absorbed. The leftover parts are turned into... poo!

⑤ Why do I need to poo?

To get rid of the bits that your body doesn't need. These parts are squashed together and mixed with dead cells and water from your gut. They leave your body when you go to the toilet.

What is my skeleton made of?

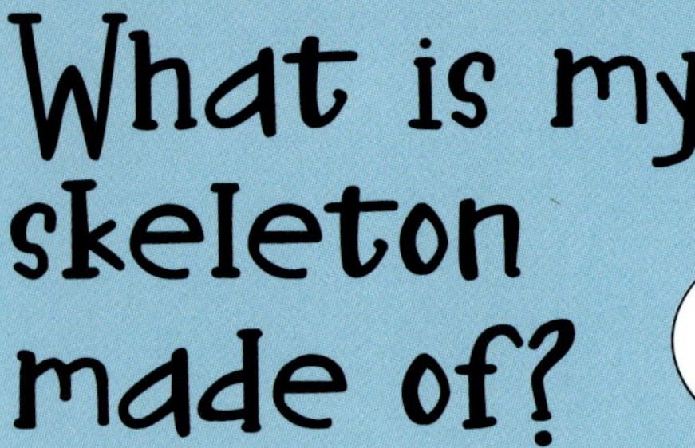

Imagine how floppy and blobby you'd be without bones!

Bones form the rigid framework for your body—your skeleton. They support your body and provide somewhere for your muscles to fix to.

Skull
Clavicle
Jaw
Ribs
Humerus
Sternum
Spine
Ulna
Radius
Pelvis
Femur
Patella
Fibula
Tibia
Phalanges

How do muscles move me?

Most muscles are fixed to your bones. As they contract, they pull the bones along with them, moving your body. Being active makes your muscles strong. Run, swim, jump, cycle, —do anything you like!

Biceps muscle contracts to bend your arm.
contract
relax
Tendon attaches muscle to bone.
Triceps muscle relaxes.

Which muscle works the hardest?
Your heart works harder than any other muscle. It never stops pumping blood around your body throughout your life.
I need exercise too! It helps to make me strong.
Knee joint
Ankle joint
Activities like dancing are good for getting your heart working.
Hip joint
Joints make you flexible, you couldn't move without them.
How does my body bend?
You have lots of joints in your body such as in your knees, elbows, shoulders, ankles, and wrists. These are places where bones meet, and they allow your body to bend or move in different ways.
Elbow joint
Wrist joint

What happens when I breathe?

When you breathe in, your lungs fill with air. Oxygen from the air goes into your blood and is delivered to your whole body. Old air is pushed out when you breathe out.

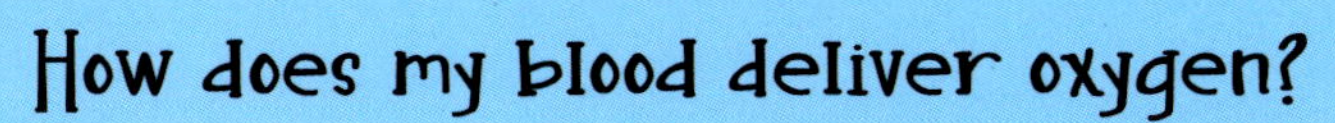

How does my blood deliver oxygen?

Your blood flows through tubes called blood vessels. These reach every single part of your body to make sure you have all the oxygen you need. Your heart and blood together are called the circulatory system.

Blood vessels

Why does my heart thump?

When you exercise, your heart beats faster to pump blood around your body quickly, to deliver the oxygen your muscles need. You also breathe faster to get more oxygen, and you feel out of breath.

Why can't I breathe underwater?

Because you don't have gills like a fish! Your lungs can only take oxygen from the air. A fish's gills can take dissolved oxygen from water. When you swim underwater, you need to come to the surface for air.

Why am I ticklish?

Because you have a sense of touch! Your body uses five senses to find out about the world around you. Your senses pick up information and send it to your brain.

Cells in your nose help you recognize smells.

Eyes let in light to help you see all around you.

Ears pick up sound vibrations to help you hear.

Special areas on your tongue tell you what something tastes like.

Skin is packed with touch sensors to help you feel.

Why can't I see in the dark?

Because you need light to bounce off objects and into your eyes. A lens in your eye helps focus the light, and a nerve carries information to your brain to make an image—and that is what you see.

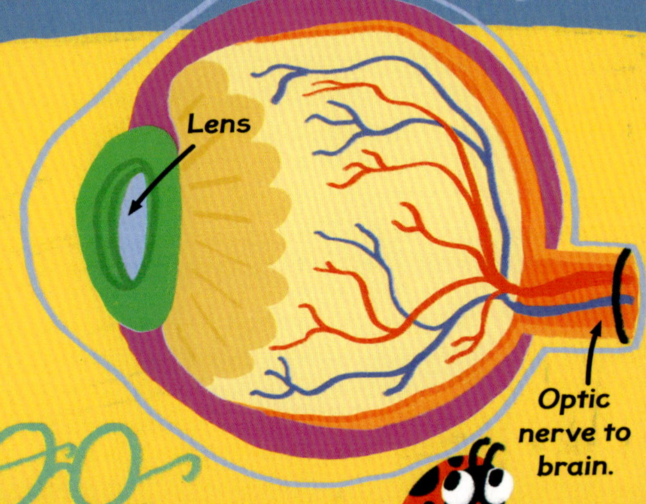

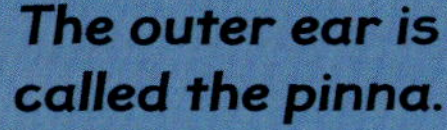

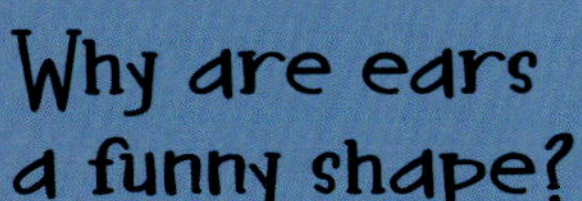

Why are ears a funny shape?

The shape of your ears helps to funnel sound into them. Sound is then carried inside your ear, where signals are sent along a nerve to your brain, so it can make sense of what you hear.

How do I smell?

Your sense of smell is produced by cells high above and behind your nose. Tiny particles of the thing you are smelling reach those cells.

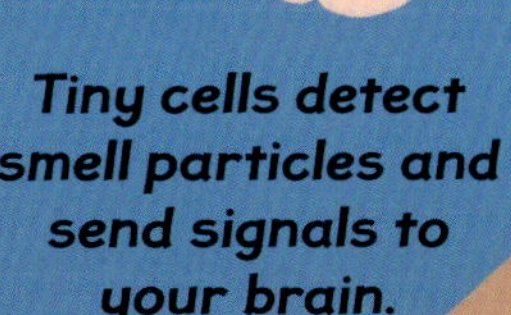

What helps me taste food?

Your tongue is covered with blobs surrounded by tiny taste buds. The taste buds send messages to your brain about the chemicals dissolved in food, and your brain turns the information into tastes.

Is my brain in charge?

What you say, think, and how you move, and everything else you do, is controlled by your brain.

It receives information

A network of nerves tells your brain what is happening to your body. Your brain is linked to your body by your spinal cord.

It sends messages

Your brain sends messages to your body, telling it how to react or move.

What do my nerves do?

Nerves are collections of nerve cells (neurons). They carry information between all parts of your body and brain. When you see, smell, taste, or hear anything, information is carried by nerves to your brain super-quickly.

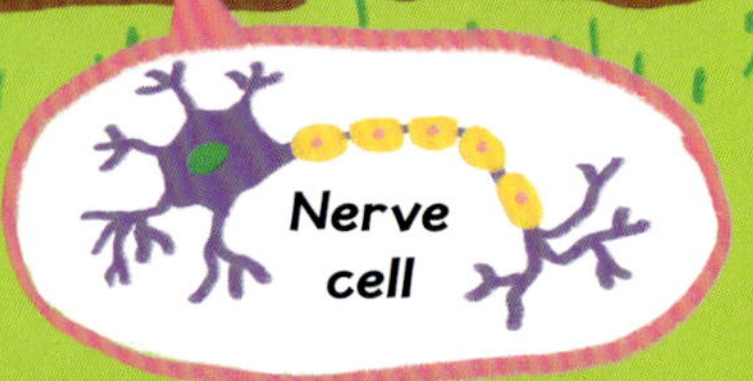

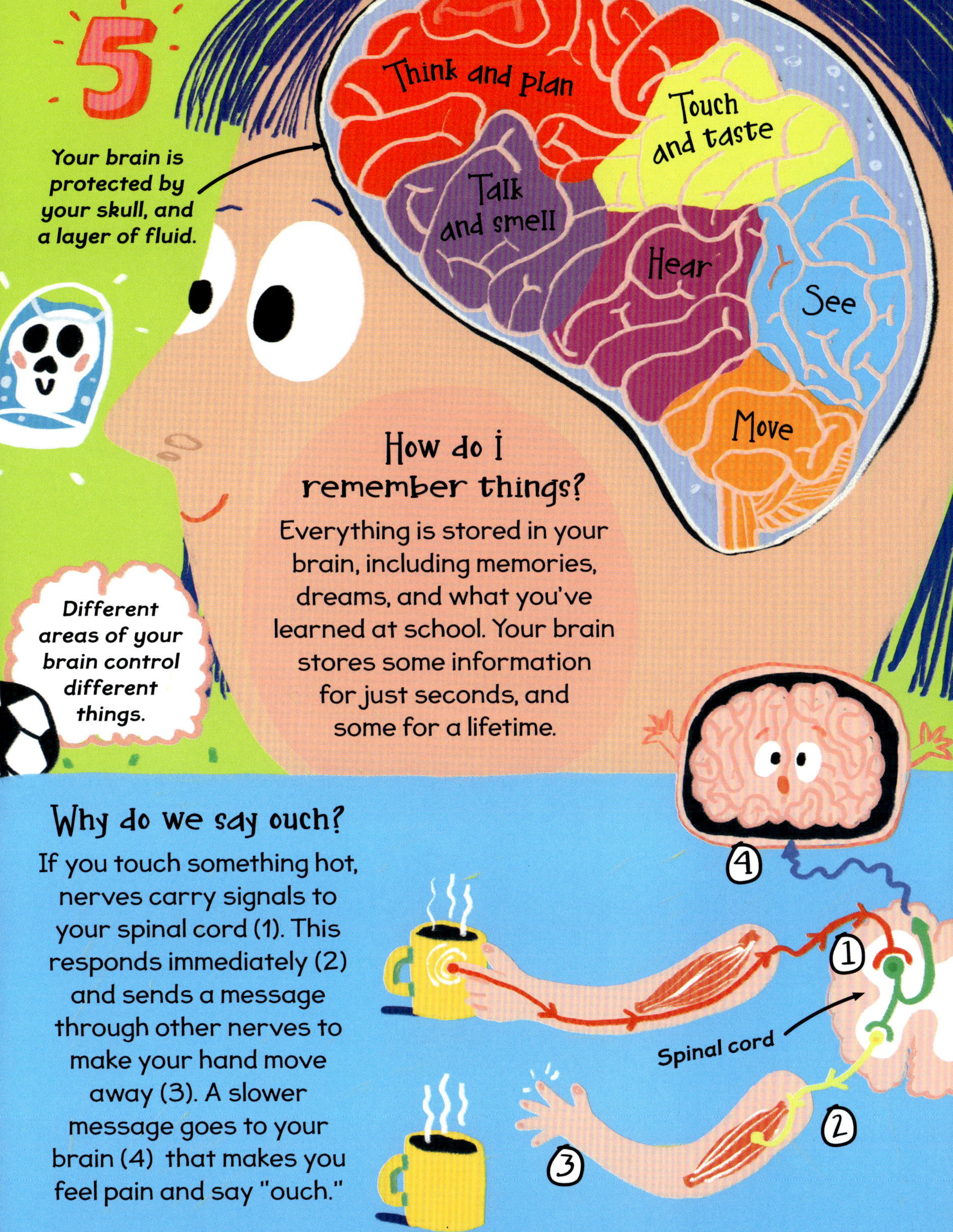

How do I remember things?

Everything is stored in your brain, including memories, dreams, and what you've learned at school. Your brain stores some information for just seconds, and some for a lifetime.

Why do we say ouch?

If you touch something hot, nerves carry signals to your spinal cord (1). This responds immediately (2) and sends a message through other nerves to make your hand move away (3). A slower message goes to your brain (4) that makes you feel pain and say "ouch."

Where do babies come from?

Babies come from inside their mom's body. A baby grows in the mom's uterus, where it gets everything it needs until it's ready to be born.

Goodness from the mother's food is carried along the cord to the baby.

Egg cell divides again and again.

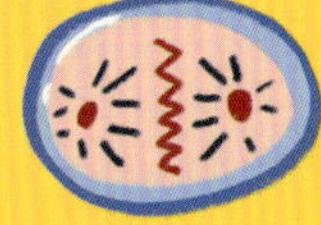

How fast does a baby grow?

Inside its mom, a baby grows really fast. It starts off as a tiny egg, which divides to make the billions of cells that make up the whole baby. After nine months, the baby is big enough to be born.

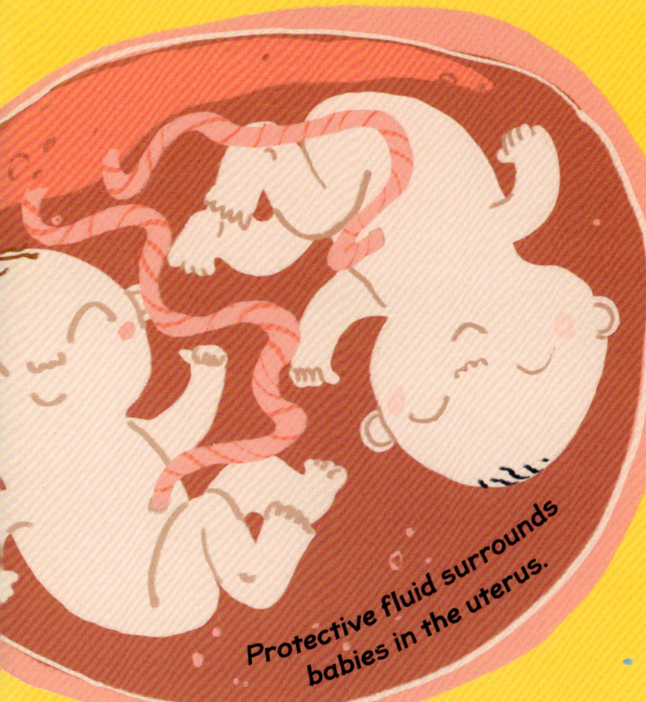

Can there be more than one baby?

If two eggs grow, or if one egg splits in half, there can be two babies—twins. Twins from two eggs look different, but twins from the same egg are identical.

WAAAH!
WAAH!

32 weeks
16.5 inches

40 weeks
20 inches

Why do babies cry?

When babies are born, they can't talk or do anything for themselves. They cry to tell their parents that they're hungry or cold—or that their diaper needs changing!

A compendium of questions

Why do my first teeth fall out?

Your first teeth are temporary—you have them until your mouth grows large enough for your permanent teeth. You have 20 first teeth, and they are replaced by larger, stronger, teeth.

What are hiccups?

If the muscle across your chest suddenly squeezes, it can snap shut the opening to your vocal flaps, making the "hic" sound.

Why do we like sugar if it's bad for us?

Millions of years ago, our ancestors ate a sugar-rich fruit diet. So gradually people grew to like sweet things.

Why do i yawn?

No one's quite sure, but possibly as a way of getting more oxygen into your body quickly.

What are goosebumps?

They are bumps on your skin where tiny muscles make your hairs stand up if you are cold or scared.

Why do we get wrinkles?

As skin ages, it loses its elasticity, so it can't spring back into shape after stretching (such as when you smile).

Why don't I have to remember to breathe?

Your brain deals with all kinds of automatic activities without you having to think about them, including breathing and digesting food.

What is my belly button for?

When you were inside your mother, you got nutrients and oxygen through the umbilical cord that connected you to her body. The belly button is what's left after the cord is cut.

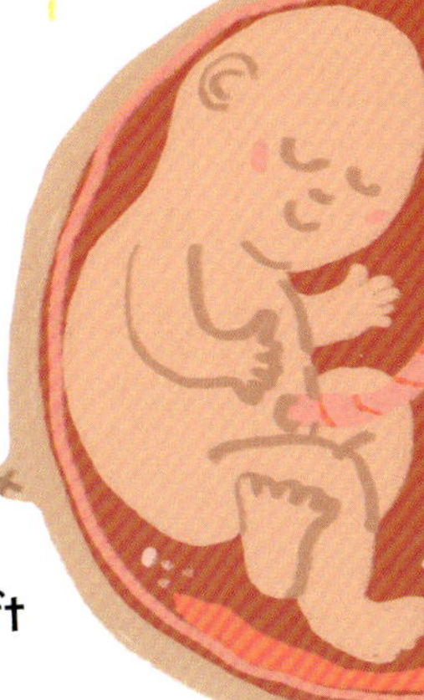

Why is blood red?

Blood contains a chemical for carrying oxygen that contains iron. When this chemical picks up oxygen, it turns redder.

What makes a scab?

When your blood meets the air, special cells called platelets break up and mix with a protein in blood to make tangly fibers, forming a scab.

Why do I sleep more when I'm ill?

Your body needs energy to fight the illness, so to save energy it makes you sleep.

SCIENCE

We know about the world around us because scientists look carefully and carry out experiments. You could be a scientist! All you have to do is...

① Spot a problem

Keep your eyes and ears open. Look out for questions to ask and problems to solve.

② Have an idea

Think of something that could explain or solve the problem. This is your theory.

③ Design an experiment

Work out how to test your idea—an experiment. Change just one thing at a time to make a fair test.

④ Check what happens

Were you right? If not, you might need a new theory and a new experiment.

3

Cider

Oranges and lemons

Sea water

It's worth a try...

Vinegar

Lind chose six pairs of sick sailors. All had the same food, except he gave each pair one extra thing.

Why do we need scientists?

The work of scientists can make life better. A discovery can lead to more questions and experiments. Science keeps on going.

Modern scientists found out that it is the Vitamin C in fruit that stops scurvy.

How does electricity get to my house?

Electricity is a type of energy. It is generated in power plants then carried along a network of cables, all the way to the wires and electrical sockets throughout your house.

How is electricity made?

We get electricity by changing other forms of energy such as sunlight, wind, moving water, or by burning coal, oil, or gas.

Coal, oil, and gas are known as fossil fuels, because they come from the remains of animals and plants that lived long ago. A lot of our energy comes from burning fossil fuels.

Wires inside the walls carry electricity to all the places it's needed. We plug electrical objects into sockets in the wall.

Fossil fuels will run out in the future, and burning them causes pollution. So people are trying to use more energy from sources that can't be used up.

Solar power

Energy from sunlight is captured in solar panels and changed into electricity.

Water power

The energy of water held by a dam is changed into electrical energy.

Wind power

Wind turbines change the wind's movement energy into electricity.

Why do I have a shadow?

Your body blocks light coming from the Sun or a lamp, making a darker patch on the other side.

Why is my reflection the wrong way round?

Light from the left side of your body travels to the mirror and bounces off, making the left side of your reflection.

What makes a rainbow?

If sunlight (white light) passes through raindrops at the right angle, it is split up into a spectrum of colors inside the raindrops. The colors come out in different directions.

You see one color from each raindrop—which color depends on the angle you are looking at the raindrop. All together they make a rainbow!

Why can't I see around corners?

Light always travels in straight lines. You can see around corners, but only if you bounce the light around a bit using mirrors. This is how a periscope in a submarine works.

Why do things fall?

The force of gravity pulls objects toward the center of the Earth—downward! Gravity is everywhere in the Universe, pulling things with less mass toward things with more mass. The Earth has more mass than anything on it.

Things only move if a force acts on them. You can think of forces as "pushes" or "pulls." I'm falling because gravity is pulling me down.

Drag

Gravity

Why does a parachute slow your fall?

A force called drag acts on the parachute. When the parachute opens, air is trapped under it. The air has to be pushed out of the way for the parachute to fall. The air holds the parachute up while gravity pulls it down.

How does a magnet stick your picture to the fridge?

Some metals are magnetic (they will stick to a magnet). Magnetism is a force that can act even through thin layers that are not magnetic—like paper.

Which force stops you from slipping?

Friction is a force between surfaces that stops them sliding over each other. On ice, there is very little friction. There is more between rough surfaces, so your shoes grip to a rough road surface, but slip on ice.

Which force pushes up?

Buoyancy! Buoyancy is a force that pushes upward through a fluid (such as water or air) against the weight of an object. When the weight pushing down (gravity) and the buoyancy are equal, the object doesn't move up or down.

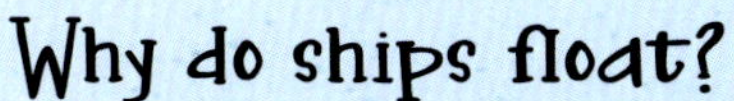

Why do ships float?

Whether something sinks or floats depends on its density (how heavy something is for its volume). Most big ships are made of metal. Metal is more dense than water, but a ship floats because it is mostly full of air.

Do fish sink or float?

They can do both! Fish are almost the same density as water. Many types have a swim bladder, which is a sac filled with gas in their stomach. The amount of gas controls the fish's buoyancy to keep it at the right level in the water. It can add more gas to go up, or lose gas to go down.

What is matter?

Matter is everything around you! It has three states: a solid, a liquid, or a gas.

Why does ice cream melt?

Materials change state as they heat up or cool down. Heating a solid above its melting point turns it to liquid. The melting point for ice cream is 32° Fahrenheit.

To keep ice cream frozen solid, we store it in the freezer.

How does a liquid become a gas?

Heating a liquid to its boiling point turns it to a gas. The boiling point of water is 212° Fahrenheit.

Melting and boiling are reversible. If you cool a gas below its boiling point it becomes liquid again. And if you cool a liquid below its melting point it becomes solid.

Not all things melt when heated. Some just burn. Which of these things do you think would melt?

- Woolly sweater
- Egg
- Glass bottle
- Sausage
- Toffee
- Metal key
- Book
- Wooden chair

Answer:
glass, toffee, and metal melt

How many?

320
The number of days it would take to drive to the Moon nonstop at 30 miles per hour.
60–70
The percentage of your body that is water.
186,000
The speed in miles per second that light travels.
3%
How much taller an astronaut is in space where gravity is not pulling their body downward.
A skydiver can reach a speed of 120 miles per hour.
50%
The proportion of cells in your body that are not you, but germs and other micro organisms.
1,000,000,000,000,000,000,000,000
Roughly how many stars there are in the known Universe.

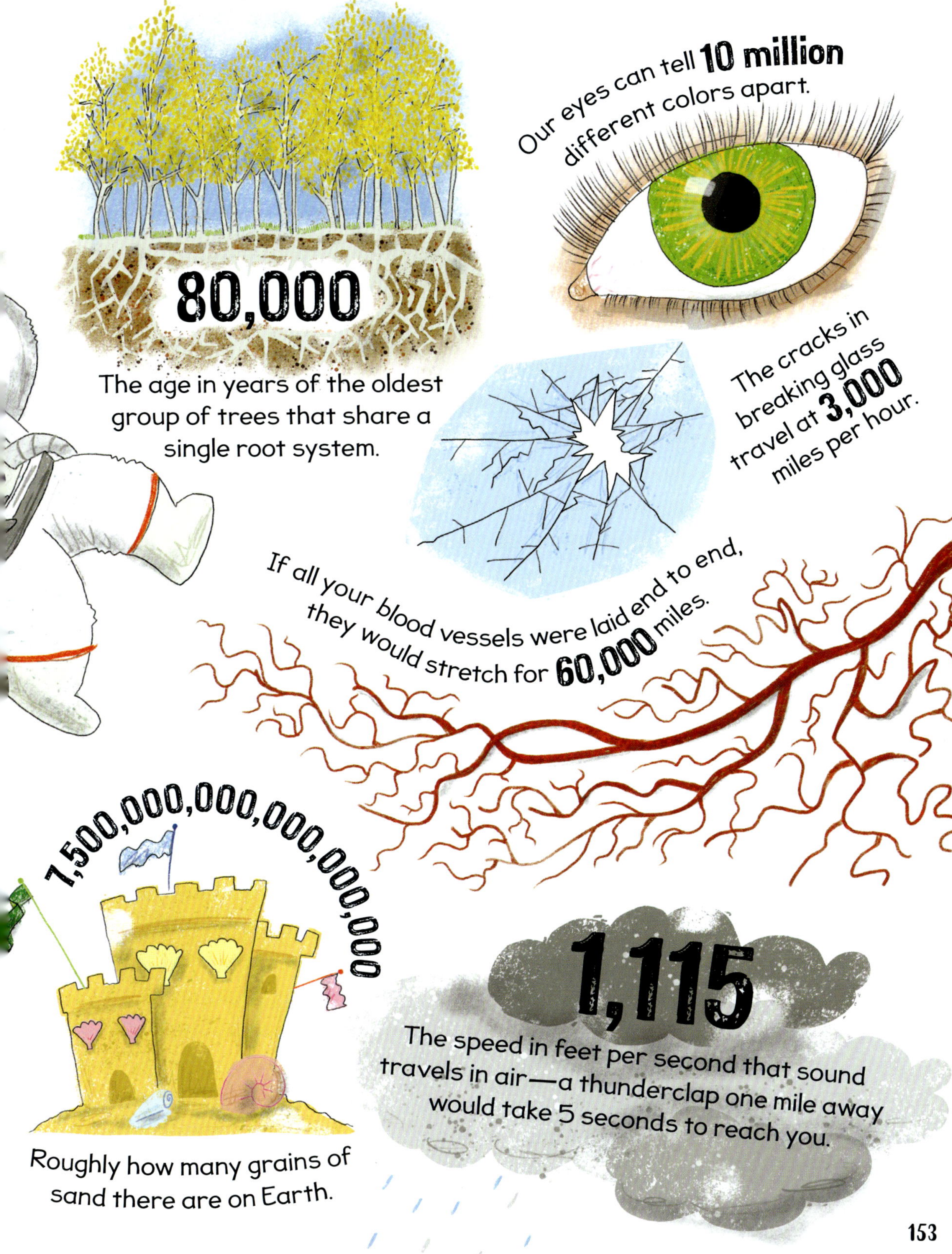

80,000
The age in years of the oldest group of trees that share a single root system.
Our eyes can tell 10 million different colors apart.
The cracks in breaking glass travel at 3,000 miles per hour.
If all your blood vessels were laid end to end, they would stretch for 60,000 miles.
7,500,000,000,000,000,000
Roughly how many grains of sand there are on Earth.
1,115
The speed in feet per second that sound travels in air—a thunderclap one mile away would take 5 seconds to reach you.

Would you rather?

Would you rather invent an amazing new **material** or design a fantastic **vehicle**?
Would you rather be **super-stretchy** like elastic, or **super-springy** and bounce everywhere?
Time for adventure! Would you rather be an **astronaut** going to Mars or a **diver** exploring the deepest oceans?
Would you rather be so **light** you can walk on water...
...or so **dense** you could walk along the seabed?

index

E

F

G

H

T

U

V

W

XY